To Mrs. E[...]
Family Member,

May the unlimited Grace of
God shine upon you as
you read this Book!

"Jesus Saves
~THAT~
None Perish!!"

From your dear Family Member,

Zallu Z.[signature]
08/31/2021

THE CATASTROPHE IN THE GARDEN

ZOLLIE L. SMITH

WESTBOW
PRESS®
A DIVISION OF THOMAS NELSON
& ZONDERVAN

This book is a work of non-fiction. Unless otherwise noted, the author and the publisher make no explicit guarantees as to the accuracy of the information contained in this book and in some cases, names of people and places have been altered to protect their privacy.

WestBow Press books may be ordered through booksellers or by contacting:

WestBow Press
A Division of Thomas Nelson & Zondervan
1663 Liberty Drive
Bloomington, IN 47403
www.westbowpress.com
844-714-3454

Because of the dynamic nature of the Internet, any web addresses or links contained in this book may have changed since publication and may no longer be valid. The views expressed in this work are solely those of the author and do not necessarily reflect the views of the publisher, and the publisher hereby disclaims any responsibility for them.

Any people depicted in stock imagery provided by Getty Images are models, and such images are being used for illustrative purposes only.
Certain stock imagery © Getty Images.

Scripture quotations marked (ESV) are from The ESV® Bible (The Holy Bible, English Standard Version®), copyright © 2001 by Crossway, a publishing ministry of Good News Publishers. Used by permission. All rights reserved.

Scripture marked (KJV) taken from the King James Version of the Bible.

Scripture marked (NKJV) taken from the New King James Version®. Copyright © 1982 by Thomas Nelson. Used by permission. All rights reserved.

Scripture quotations marked (NLT) are taken from the Holy Bible, New Living Translation, copyright ©1996, 2004, 2015 by Tyndale House Foundation. Used by permission of Tyndale House Publishers, Carol Stream, Illinois 60188. All rights reserved.

ISBN: 978-1-6642-3821-3 (sc)
ISBN: 978-1-6642-3822-0 (hc)
ISBN: 978-1-6642-3820-6 (e)

Library of Congress Control Number: 2021912737

Print information available on the last page.

WestBow Press rev. date: 7/17/2021

ENDORSEMENTS

"The author, Rev. Zollie Smith, has always been an advocate for broken and lost humanity. I have had the privilege of serving Zollie during the ten years he was president of the National Black Fellowship of the Assemblies of God, and his 10 years as the Executive Director of U.S. Missions. He has never steered from that passion. **The Catastrophe in the Garden** will awaken and enlighten you to the depth of God's love and purpose for you – confirming He has an assignment for your life. It's not an assignment for you to determine, it's one for you to discover. Once discovered, the Spirit empowers us to develop it for His glory. Ephesians 2:10 declares, "we are his workmanship created in Christ Jesus unto good works which he planned in advance for us to do". The only hope for humanity is the good news that Jesus saves! **The Catastrophe in the Garden** reveals how sin separates us from our Heavenly Father and our divine purpose. We sin because we do not know our identity as God's children in Christ. Zollie will assist you in gaining that perspective in your journey through, **The Catastrophe in the Garden**"

Rev. Malcolm Burleigh, Executive Director of US Missions Assemblies of God. Served as the President of the National Black Fellowship, Senior Pastor of Living Faith, Peninsular Florida District presbyter and Author.

"My friend Zollie has skillfully taken the creation story, combined it with his life experiences and has shown us God's heart for humanity...LOVE.

Reading this book will remind you about the great lengths that a loving Heavenly Father endured to have an intimate relationship with you.

Thanks Zollie for sharing the grace of Gods transformation in your life and reminding us that, "we are His workmanship created in Christ Jesus"

Rev. Doug Clay, General Superintendent Assemblies of God,
Springfield, MO
Author

"In The Catastrophe in the Garden Zollie Smith walks us through the story of Creation, the amazing systems that God the Father put in place and how through our savior we can get back on track. This book will bring revelation and understanding to many of your deepest questions."

Rev. Jeff Hartensveld AGWM Regional Director Asia Pacific,
Assemblies of God
Springfield, MO
Author

"Zollie is a life architect. He seeks to build people by establishing them upon the foundation of truth, God's moral and biblical truth. He is uniquely qualified as he has lived by biblical systems and principles as long as I have known him. His lifestyle of leadership by example clearly comes through his newest book, The Catastrophe in the Garden. In it, you the reader will come face to face with the greatest story ever told, the gospel of Jesus Christ. Zollie's aim is that none would perish but instead experience the abundant life that God, the Creator, purposed by designed. You will be blessed by this book as you align your life story with His story (the story of Jesus Christ)."

Bishop Walter F. Harvey President, National Black Fellowship (Assemblies of God) Executive Director, WI+H Movement, Author

It has been near 12 years since the first time I met Zollie Smith. I was a new employee in U.S. Missions, and he was the Executive Director. It took only a few moments to discern his pastoral heart, his genuine interest in people, and his passion to know what a person's relationship is with the Lord. He truly wants to know, "What is your story?" Now, taking a deep dive into his personal story, I can see that it has all been part of a story that is much bigger than any of us. His story, my story, your story. We are all interdependent on one another, and Zollie explains it so well as he draws us into the heart of knowing God. So, he asks, "How does your story align with the story of God?" As you turn the pages In **The Catastrophe in the Garden**, the answer will become crystal clear. It all began "in the beginning." And it all began in the garden. It is like reading the account of Genesis for the first time, with new eyes.

Qené Manon Jeffers, Administrative Assistant U.S.
Missions, Assemblies of God, Springfield, MO, Author

"Zollie is my friend. **The <u>Catastrophe in the Garden</u>** is a historically, gripping narrative of the root ills of society and the misdeeds of individuals. However, Creator God makes a way for individuals to be re-created so that society has the possibility of being transformed."

Rev. Dr. Greg Mundis, Assemblies of God World
Missions Director Springfield, MO, Author

"The Catastrophe in the Garden is most definitely a must read....a resourceful book full of important information on the Biblical account of God's creation. Zollie Smith in his brilliance show us how God chose us to be a key asset for the good of His creation, because we are a vital part of its story."

Rev. Michael Nelson is the Senior Pastor of Praise Tabernacle, a District Presbyter of The Penn Florida District, and former president of The National Black Fellowship

"Wow! What a journey. My friend of over 25 years has written an amazing book that begins in the Garden of Eden and takes the reader through every aspect of life, leaving no stone unturned. Zollie begins by exegeting the scriptures within their historical context, immediately transplants them into the everyday lives of readers, thereby permeating the spiritual growth of twenty first century men and women.

The journey culminates with what Zollie calls "My Story Framed by the Creation Story." One is gripped with intensified anticipation as he recounts how his life was spared as he experienced the horrors of war. His painful experience leaps from the pages as he narrates side-by-side proximity with his friends becoming casualties of the Vietnam War, while becoming a casualty himself.

Zollie an ambassador for Christ for nearly all his life gives clear understanding as to why God protected him and moved him to write this tremendous book.

The Catastrophe in the Garden is loaded with living, powerful and sharp scriptural references and will positively change your life forever."

Rev. DR. Charles Sanderfur is a National Board-Certified Life and Executive Coach with the Center for Credentialing and Education, a Nationally Certified Psychotherapist and holds ordination credentials with the Assemblies of God USA. Author

"REV. Zollie Smith does an amazing job of getting to the root of humanities ills in **The Catastrophe in the Garden**. He brings a complete perspective on how Satan is working behind the scenes to disrupt the order of God. He also shows us how and why Jesus Christ is the only hope for all of humanity. A must read!"

Rev. Samuel Soto is Senior Pastor of Powerhouse Christian Center Sectional Officer, New Jersey District Assemblies of God

"With riveting spiritual vigor and insight, Zollie the Author, has dissected the Creation Account using scripture to validate, testify with supporting scripture. The depth of this spiritual filled book leaves one uplifted with hope. The reader can readily see the significance of the author's penmanship in his quest to help all of God's children understand their value to God and His merciful grace, reasoning and detail care He took in creating the world we call home (Earth and the heavens).

The Author's spiritual knowledge vividly leads the reader through the continuum of events that led man and woman to make such a regrettable choice that has had irreparable misery and damage to all creation. For many parishioners, skeptics and non-believers, the question on the validity and sanctity of creation will have eternal life consequences. The author has shown in-dept chronological proof that God "IS" and did indeed create not only this world but the universe in totality. Praise God for His wonderful saving grace that one day soon mankind's arch enemy (Satan) will no longer cause any misery to God's creation, especially to those who believe in Him.

I encourage all of God's children (no matter what religious tenor one may have) to read this book and take heed to what the author has so eloquently, spiritually and prayerfully presented. God will re-establish the purity of Earth, after our sinful existence. Why not take advantage of what the author has labored to convey, heaven or hell awaits your decision NOW – time is not on our side, how say ye?"

Rev. Dr James White, PhD, Teacher, Preacher and Writer.

"Dr. Zollie Smith is a gifted leader with a pastor's heart. He has the uncanny ability to unite spiritual truth with strategic thinking. **The Catastrophe in the Garden** provides the salvation narrative within this thought process. He clearly demonstrates that such themes are biblical and should be embraced by all who are called to lead. The Catastrophe in the Garden is a great read! Dr. Zollie systemically demonstrates that, God, is in fact, the ultimate strategist! While reading, my heart was filled with prayer, worship, and joy at the intentionality our Heavenly Father reflected in His salvation plan. I whole heartedly recommend The Catastrophe in the Garden!"

Dr. Darnell K. Williams, Lead Pastor, One Church
Lima Vice President, National Black Fellowship of the
Assemblies of God Assemblies of God Non-Resident
Executive Presbyter (Language Area, Other) Publisher

This book is respectfully dedicated to some of the greatest people God created

Amanda Smith my beloved mother who raised me in the Church. Her love of God transcended in her loving me and my siblings sacrificially. As a single parent she poured into us the value of God in our lives and we should show our gratitude by being the best at what we did. She was a true provider with little resources but she always made sure we were taken care of. She loved her children and I am a product of her selfless sacrifices. Mother your labor was not in vain.

Parrie Lee White my beloved grand mom who taught me the value of daily intense prayer and Bible study. Momma is who I called her was a symbol of righteousness and holiness. She personified order and decency. She was not a formally educated lady but you would not know that by her ability to communicate very well and portray the demeanor of a dignitary without a title. She was neat, and consistently in control of her life, surroundings and grands. I was blessed to have her as one of my key role models. She invested in me by just being an awesome loving and caring grand mom who was not ashamed to live her life for God. Momma your godly life was the foundation for my loving God.

Zollie Smith my beloved father who lovingly made up for the 25 years we were separated. That is a statement I make without reservations. Due to reasons out of his control, he was unable to raise me in person. However, when we finally met he made know at that very moment he loved me and was proud to be my dad. It was a miracle from God. Although we had never seen one another it appeared we were never separated. He and I became best of friends and enjoyed one another immensely. Yes, he was a Christian. We made sure of that. He poured into my life with child support monthly, he sent gifts for Christmas and we wrote one another occasionally. I imagine that is why it felt we were father and son. God was gracious to provide us with 37 joyous years together. Dad your confident and caring heart for people and your commitment in fulfilling your obligations made a major impact in my life. You taught me to be responsible in your loving caring way.

Mr. Johnny Kate my beloved mentor and life coach. Mr. Johnny and I met in an orange grove picking fruit. I was about 15 years of age and he was in his mid 60's. He was a loner so one day at lunch break I went over to talk with him and we hit it off immediately. He appeared to be non-relational but it turned out he was a very friendly and wise man. From that time until I relocated to New Jersey Mr. Johnny was my mentor. He taught me construction work, how to operate a power mower, how to be respectful as a young man and not make a fool of myself. His mentoring and watching his television which we did not have at the time, was rich and fulfilling for me because it gave me time with a wise man that enjoyed my friendship at his age. He was an avid baseball and wrestling fan. After I moved to New Jersey and I told him I was a pastor he wrote me a letter with a sermon to preach entitled "You have got to make it home." The sermon focused on baseball his favorite pass time. He stated it is good to get a base hit but that will not get you home. You need someone else to get hits so you can get home. In other words life takes a team effort to get home to God. That message was for me Mr. Johnny, because your hits in my life helped get me home to Jesus.

Corporal William Franks my beloved hero. Franks and I were in B Company of the 101st Airborne Division in Vietnam. Franks and I became friends immediately upon my arrival to the unit. He was a friendly warm-hearted individual. We would converse daily, and his character and conduct were nothing like the rest of us. I never heard him use profanity or engage in outlandish conversations. He was so straight I introduced him to my 1st cousin Katheren as a pin pal. They communicated and he would greet me with a smile when she wrote. On the darkest day of my life around 5PM we were air lifted into the jungle of Lam Dong Province where shortly after landing and entering the tree line we were ambushed. As a result, I was wounded and while on the ground bleeding in pain pinned down by the enemy, Franks came to assist me when he suffered wounds to his body and was killed in action (KIA). Prior to falling to the ground our eyes locked on one another and he appeared to say, "I am sorry I cannot help you, Smithy." Had Franks not shown up I would not have written this book. By coming to my aide he drew the enemy's gunfire from me to him. I am convinced Franks was a Child of God and is at home with God. Franks, you did help me friend by demonstrating the sacrificial act of saving a friend who was in dire trouble. Your death lived out the reality of the sacrifice Jesus made for me. And your death is memorialized through my life, I see and think about you all the time my friend, Rest In Peace for there is no need to be sorry.

There are many others who contributed to my life story—They are remembered!

CONTENTS

The earth is the LORD's, and everything in it. The world and all its people belong to him. For he laid the earth's foundation on the seas and built it on the ocean depths. (Psalm 24:1–2)

PREFACE

My love for God and His great supernatural plan of salvation through His beloved son Jesus Christ, completely transformed my life and the lives of many others who put their faith in Him. God's salvation plan is the only means of rescuing perishing souls from eternal damnation. The plan is strategically put in place to transform humankind from death to life in Jesus Christ. The only requirement is to believe in Jesus by accepting Him as your Lord and Savior.

My heart is grieved with pain over the acts of inhumanity perpetrated by humankind against humankind. When we include the self-imposed addictions, such as alcohol, drugs, pornography, cigarettes and personal human neglect or abuses, my heart becomes heavy with grief and compassion knowing those who do such things will be cast into the lake of fire with Satan forever as stated in Revelation 21:8. Racial hatred, along with class and gender hatred, is sadistic and incomprehensible for me to rationalize since we all are descendants of Noah's family, eight people, four couples. I restrain myself from over watching the news reports because they are filled with sadistic acts of violence displayed by human beings against each other. We are continuously bombarded with other causes of death due to the many health issues alone. Could you imagine what the world would be like if we followed God's truths anchored in love for one another?

By adding the value of self-worth and resourcing those who are struggling with life and see no way out, they can and must be rescued through acts of compassion. These actions could vastly curtail the deadly addictions and criminal behaviors, the culprits of many deaths. Dysfunctional lifestyles contribute largely to the world's health problems. We invest billions of dollars researching for cures caused by self-imposed addictions that would not exist if people would love themselves enough to abstain from their use. Humankind discovers and invent ways to kill themselves, such as alcohol, nicotine, illicit drugs, pornography and etc., for money and the hope of escaping the mental stresses of life. Many use addictive substances, some legalized, to cope with their troubled lives, not realizing they are compounding their troubles. At the same time humankind works tirelessly to discover ways to cure the ailments caused by the addictive substances. That sounds like a circle of confusion to me. Could you imagine if the monies wasted on addictive debilitating substances was converted to feeding the hungry, educating everyone, adding value to everyone through giving a hand up by training them for a good paying profession, which would likely contribute toward helping in stabilizing the world. Those acts are humanitarian and ordered by God. They provide temporary relief for those struggling with life challenges. However, they become pathways to the hearts of our fellowman in need. In essence everyone needs deliverance from their sins and the curse of death. There is only one source who is qualified to meet that need and it is Jesus the Savior. You see I believe it is possible for everyone to experience the abundant life by following God's transformational plan of salvation which was purchased through Jesus Christ for all of humanity. Yes, we will still die and suffer under the curses God placed upon humankind for their sins but we will endure because of our guaranteed future of eternal life God provided through Jesus Christ. Therefore the only hope for humankind is the Good News that Jesus Saves. We need laborers to share the Good News of Jesus with our fellowman that none perish.

I have been inspired by the Holy Spirit to write this book to challenge the child of God to draw closer to God by falling in love with Him over and over again daily as your Heavenly Father. To identify yourself as God's loving born again child. To become committed as a laborer of Christ full of compassion for those that are perishing. To become a bold witness of Jesus Christ, so your love for Him will not be self-contained but it will flow from your heart to others. To fellowship with the Holy Spirit daily so you can freely be led by Him to become a difference maker for all of humanity. Therefore you will value what God values (Souls) and see where He is working so you can join Him. God desires to use you to bring freedom to fellow human beings from the power of sin and death through sharing your life story of how you replaced evil for good through Jesus Christ.

It is my desire that this book will challenge you to become God's beacon of light in a perishing world that none perish by sharing your victorious life story anchored in Jesus Christ, your Savior! Please remember, everyone is important, everyone significant and everyone is your blessing; therefore, no one can be left behind!

May the Holy Spirit minister to you as you read The Catastrophe in the Garden.

ACKNOWLEDGEMENTS

First and foremost, I am blessed and privileged to have God as my beloved Heavenly Father, His son Jesus as my elder brother, and the Holy Spirit as my confidant and teacher. I realize without reservations that I am who I am by the grace of my loving Heavenly Father. The more God reveals Himself to me through His truths the more I behold His unlimited mercy and grace for me. He is the greatest of anything or anyone I can identify with in this world. I am amazed over His creative geniuses of making interdependent, unified functional structures that operate orderly and decently; of which I am one. To God be the GLORY!

I acknowledge my wife Phyllis who God gave me as my earthly soul mate. Phyllis and I have been married for 51 years and the first seven years were extremely rough on her due to my riotous lifestyle. She endured me despite me. Phyllis is a faithful and loving wife. She is very discipline and demands it of me. She became a born-again Child of God after our 7th year of marriage and persuaded me to give my life back to God. God answered her prayers and I responded. That act made me realize how much she loved me. Phyllis is a very gifted and creative woman, wife and mother. She is the anchor that held our family together as a pastor's wife and during my years in a demanding career in law enforcement. On many occasions she wore two hats, mine and hers and she wore them with excellence. Raising six daughters never pressured her. She would sew their clothing as needed, transport them to their school events while operating an in-home childcare center. She is my "wonder" wife. I am amazed how powerfully strong her trust is in God which has enabled her to pour out her love for me our daughters, grandchildren, and sons-in-law. She has a bond to our daughters that is awesome to behold. They chatter and text like teenagers enjoying one another daily and the grands as well. Their loving relationship adds value to me in knowing that God provided me with a good wife who is my good-thing. Phyllis my love, thanks for the glorious presence you are in my life story. I love you!

I also acknowledge my six daughters Carnetha, Eboni, Kellie, Crystal, Ashley and Zol-Licia, for their loving respect and obedience to me as their father. These young ladies are not perfect but they have honored me and their mother. They have all excelled academically in their respected careers. They have not made me ashamed to be their father. Our daughters made great sacrifices of support and commitment as pastor's kids. I did not give them enough quality time to be their dad because of my demands as a pastor and in my secular profession. There was always pressure upon them to conduct themselves in what is termed as a "pastor's kid." I am honored to say, they passed the test. They are not perfect, but they are my heroines forever and I love them as my precious gifts from God! Individually and collectively they have added value to my life story. I cannot forget my grandchildren they are precious as well, Anaya, J'Shon, Barrie Jr, Zollie, Roman, Paxton, Kamrea and Kayla, and one great grandson Cameron. I love you, my family, in a very special way!

I acknowledge the investment that the following institutions, their leaders and constituents played in solidifying my life story; in various ways of honoring God through Jesus Christ. I would have to write another book to name them all: God's House of Prayer, Plainfield, New Jersey (10 years); Eternal Life Christian Center, Somerset, NJ (20 years); Assemblies of God, New Jersey (19 years); President National Black Fellowship AG, U.S. (10 years); Executive Director U.S. Missions, Springfield, MO (10years); The Moore Elementary and Mickens High School teachers and school mates (12 years) and the village community of Carver Heights, Dade City, FL. To all of you, of which a large number now present in that great cloud of witnesses in heaven, I thank you for the sacrificial contributions of your time, energy, finances, and faithfulness to believe and support me and my family. I pray in some way I added value to your life story as well. You are God's gift to me, for which I say, "THANK YOU!" May God continue to smile upon you, because you were and are my difference makers!

INTRODUCTION

One sign that an individual, organization, or institution has failed to achieve its purpose for being is when people, places, and objects become dysfunctional. The key for any individual, organization, or institution is knowing its defined function. The word *function* refers to duties or activities, but there is more to it; it can apply to people, places, and objects. As an adjective, the word *functional* modifies something that achieves a desired action or outcome. Functionalism is a doctrine suggesting the function of a person, place, or object, which determines its design and composition.

The design and composition of people, places, and objects take place prior to the making or building process. The design plan must also include the interdependent functional operations of the systems working as a holistic structure. God's desired outcome was unity so that each person, place, or object would support one another so that maximum results could be achieved.

Functionality is the foundation of organizational operations. Management oversight must govern the functional operations of the person, place, or object. The most effective and logical way for this to occur requires governance directives included in the design phase. Then, it is incumbent on all to fulfill their functional roles for the success of the whole. Once noncompliance occurs, the once functional becomes dysfunctional, which results in chaos and confusion leading to the demise of the entire structure.

On our journey through the creation story, we will examine how God, the chief architect and builder, created the cosmos, all living creatures, and humankind to fulfill His desired outcomes. To tap into the full benefit of the creation story, we must take hold of this truth; the universe and humankind are not the property of an individual or individuals, an ethnic group, a country, a city, a political party, or an organization. The cosmos, earth, and everything that inhabits it are the sole property of God. He designed and made the structures—the heavens, earth, vegetation, and all living creatures, including humankind—to bring honor and glory to Himself.

Everyone benefits through the simple act of obedience and living according to God's truths. Knowledge of God's creation is key to understanding the purpose He assigned to every structure, including the human structure.

The first three chapters of Genesis highlight the foundational history of modern humanity. Appropriately identified as the creation story, it established the pathway to modern humanity. No other document can describe the history of humankind as the Bible can. I am not writing to present an apologetic approach of the Bible, because there are others with much more wisdom and insight than me whom God used to do that. My goal is to affirm that the Bible presents the clear passage between two key factors of a healthy, functional existence: order and decency. Order denotes governance, doing the right things, and governance means forming a unity through functional directives to achieve a desired outcome.

God created a functional whole for His honor and glory. He arranged everything He created into a unity of interdependent systems working together to achieve His desired outcomes, which benefit all creation. God's order represents His righteousness, and His decency represents His holiness. Order denotes governance, and decency denotes moral conduct. The two combined provide God's divine structural foundation for all creation.

Built on truth, the Bible, His operations manual for humankind, consists of His standard operating procedures and provides guidance in performing a functional, ordered, and moral lifestyle of love toward the Godhead, self, fellow humans, and all creation. The creation story communicates the heart of God in making His cosmos into a unified design of interdependent systems and subsystems working together to build functional structures so life could exist and be sustainable according to His will, divine order, and decency.

When evil entered the world, it made God's good creation, including humankind, dysfunctional. Sin caused all things to become nonconforming to God's will for them. Evil became humanity's slave master, robbing it of its functional freedom in God. True freedom will never exist under the slavery of sin. Humankind is living under the bondage of evil and God's curses in response to the devastating sin of Adam and Eve. The horrific struggles of humanity throughout the ages were nothing less than a catastrophe, but God had a plan—and we are a part of it!

To comprehend, understand, and appreciate God, we must know His creation story and how it shapes our life story. The only authentic and detailed account of the creation story is in Genesis 1–3. The uniqueness of the creation story provides us with the only factual and truthful account of how humans came into existence and occupied their habitat, earth.

You will discover why this truth has been distorted and denied throughout the ages. Upon reading this truth, you will arise and take hold of what is rightfully yours—eternal life—and escape the final blow of the catastrophe in the garden.

CHAPTER 1

The Beginning

In the beginning God created the heavens and the earth. The earth was formless and empty, and darkness covered the deep waters. And the Spirit of God was hovering over the surface of the waters. (Genesis 1:1–2)

First Day

The creation story began with God laying out the current state of the earth prior to His makeover. The word *makeover* is used because verse 1 above denotes that heaven and earth preexisted the creation story as we know it today. I am not an expert in this area, but I am persuaded that science would bear this out. It is my conviction that a prehistoric creation existed prior to the makeover of earth and the creation of humanity; data has proven that prehistoric forms of life existed prior to the creation of humanity as we know it.

God's announcement revealed that He was ready to execute His strategic plan. A major change was about to take place per His design—a creation that would honor and glorify Him throughout the ages.

The current state of the earth as described in verse 1 is crucial. It was a lifeless and empty void of deep waters covered by darkness and lacking purpose. The description shows no form of life. There was a foundation of water covered by darkness and occupying the earth but lacking order and essential functions for life to exist.

The only life in this mass of death was God's Spirit hovering over the waters; God was on the scene. God is a Spirit, and there are always spiritual and natural focal points in His creation strategy. God is a visionary, supernatural, architectural phenom with spiritual and natural components in His structures as shown throughout His creation. His desired outcomes determined what unified structural designs would be required. He designed systems and subsystems, operational components of various compositions based on their assigned functions. Their interdependent functions defined their identification and assignment to work as a unified spiritual and natural structure.

His structures are functional in every aspect to ensure that there can be no misrepresentations of their existence and purpose. They were created to function flawlessly according to His will, for His glory and honor. When His structures no longer function as designed, they become dysfunctional and can no longer bring honor and glory to Him and be called good. When created things become dysfunctional, they lead to turmoil, chaos, and confusion. This is the pathway that becomes known as sin and sin's recompense is death. Humankind most feared enemy.

Everything exists by God; the writer showed God's approval of what He had created with these words: "God saw it was GOOD" (Genesis 1:10). These words are recorded throughout the days of creation. Everything God did reflected His goodness. For goodness to be present in every aspect of His creation story, it had to portray the divine realm of God and meet His approval.

God demands order and decency in every facet of His creation, so He intentionally organized His universe to flow out of His functional purposes, the vehicle He used to design and make what He desired in the physical realm prior to speaking it into existence. He is the God of order and decency, for which His cosmos structures exist. He systematically and meticulously put in place all the interdependent functional structures necessary to fulfill His desired outcomes. So let us learn by enjoying Him at work.

Upon looking at His created earth in its dismal, lifeless state, God moved into action to create a change, a functional universe, from death to life. Let's explore the word *universe* to appreciate the strategic value of God's works. I like the definition as stated by *Merriam-Webster's*

Dictionary: a systematic whole held to arise by and persist through the direct intervention of divine power … the world of human experience … the cosmos.1 The uniqueness of God's divine power of creation came into existence through His spoken words: "Then God said …"

The releasing of God's creation plan began with Genesis 1:3 when He said, "Let there be light." Immediately, earth underwent a major change. The light immediately flexed its power and overcame the lifeless darkness. Light is superior to darkness and what it represents; it exposes what darkness hides. Darkness prevents one from clearly seeing what is present or about to come upon one. Throughout the Bible, darkness represents evil, and light represents good. "This is the message he has given us to announce to you: God is light and there is no darkness in him at all" (1 John 1:5). We will discuss the term *darkness* and the role it plays in the grand scheme of life.

> Your eye is a lamp that provides light for your body. When your eye is good, your whole body is filled with light. But when it is bad, your body is filled with darkness. (Luke 11:34)

> Jesus spoke to the people once more and said, "I am the light of the world. If you follow me, you won't have to walk in darkness, because you will have the light that leads to life." (John 8:12)

> Merriam-Webster, s.v. "app (n.), accessed September 23, 2020, http:// www.merrian-webster.com/dictionary/app.1

The scriptures reveal that light represents life, a key factor in God's new creation strategy. The first item on the agenda was eradicating darkness so life could exist. Note that darkness was not removed but was forced to make room for light—a complementary system.

To help us understand the value of light based on God's response in Genesis 1:4, we will turn to *The Preacher's Outline Sermon Bible Commentary*, which states,

> (1:4) **Light—Creation**: God saw that His creation was *good*—light fulfilled its function. The picture is that God

looked at the *light* and saw that it was *good*. The word *good* refers to the value, the purpose, and the function of something. Hence, God looked and saw that the light was *good*: it was very valuable; it fulfilled its purpose and its function. What is the purpose and function of light? Note the statement: "God divided the light from the darkness." Unless light existed—unless light was divided from darkness—the earth would be in total darkness.[1]

Light has at least five basic functions or purposes.

⇨ Light divides darkness to give some light to the earth and universe.

⇨ Light makes things grow. Life cannot exist without light. Man, animals, green plants, and algae—all are dependent upon light in order to live upon the earth. Green plants and algae convert light into energy, and they grow thereby (the process is known as photosynthesis). Without light, there would be no plants upon earth to feed man and animal. Light is an absolute essential for life and growth.

⇨ Light gives heat and warmth.

⇨ Light gives color and beauty to things.

⇨ Light enables man and animals to see; light exposes things—all the universe and all the earth—so that man and animals can see and carry out their function in a world of variety and beauty. God saw the light and knew it was <u>good</u>" because the light fulfilled its created function. The light was exactly what God had planned; it was designed and perfectly fitted for its purpose, it was profitable, and it was functioning just as God had willed. [2] What a powerful explanation of God's plan for His makeover of the universe. It is important to grasp the importance of this information because one's potential as a child of God is maximized by understanding His master plan for humanity and the world—through His divine organizational preeminence over everything.

---

[1] Leadership Ministries Worldwide. 1996. *Genesis (Chapters 1–11)* (Vol. I, p. 65). Chattanooga, TN: Leadership Ministries Worldwide.

After studying the above information, we can see the excitement and significance of God's first spoken creation command, "Let there be light." Light immediately stepped out and executed its purpose. God continued carving out His creative design by separating the light from the darkness to establish the beginning of another key asset to His masterpiece, time. They showed His pleasure when He separated the light from the darkness and called the light day and the darkness night. Here, we see the created wisdom of God at work on the first day by adding value to the darkness through the light. This insight is significant because it details how an independent component, darkness, was dysfunctional and lifeless, but when light came on the scene and complemented it, a major transformation took place on behalf of both. The name changes show the unified interdependency between the two, which made them more valuable together than they would have been separately. Unification is the heart of God; His creation is a unified, interdependent whole covered in His grace.

The night has become a major resource by providing life-sustaining energy to God's creation. Night is essential for life to exist in partnership with day in the new universe. By working together, they produce God's time sequence for all creation. Time is one of God's major functional systems in His creation; we will explore it later.

The creation strategy of God comprises spiritual (unseen) and natural (seen) components. God designed the two independent systems to work together as a whole. The two became one based on their complementary functions. God's order and decency foundation system is in place for the functional health of the whole. It completes the end of the first day with a major change in the creation story.

What a beginning to this awesome story! I trust as you read that you will see yourself as part of God's supernatural strategic plan of creation. God chose you to be a key asset for the good of His creation because you are a vital part of its story. The creation story is so compelling and demands to be embraced by those who have a heart for God, those who value their own life and the lives of others. God works tirelessly to show His love for His creation and especially His prized trophies, humankind—us.

Do you see your story aligning with God's creation story on day one? What is your takeaway from day one? Psalm 36:5–9 reads,

Your unfailing love, O LORD, is as vast as the heavens; your faithfulness reaches beyond the clouds. Your righteousness is like the mighty mountains, your justice like the ocean depths. You care for people and animals alike, O LORD. How precious is your unfailing love, O God! All humanity finds shelter in the shadow of your wings. You feed them from the abundance of your own house, letting them drink from your river of delights. For you are the fountain of life, the light by which we see.

2 Leadership Ministries Worldwide. 1996. *Genesis (Chapters 1–11)* (Vol. I, p. 65). Chattanooga, TN: Leadership Ministries Worldwide.

CHAPTER 2

Separation of the Earth and Sky

Then God said, "Let there be a space between the waters, to separate the waters of the heavens from the waters of the earth." And that is what happened. God made this space to separate the waters of the earth from the waters of the heavens. God called the space "sky." And evening passed and morning came, marking the second day. (Genesis 1:6–8)

The Second Day

Verse 6, which begins the second day of God's creation story, focuses on separating the earthly and heavenly waters. God's plan focused on the earth—a massive body of land covered by deep waters. The waters and the earth already existed but were not functional in their present states.

As essential as water is for life, order had to exist for it to function as God desired. God spoke once again: "Let there be a space between the waters, to separate the waters of the heavens from the waters of the earth." Two areas of His creation were covered by connecting waters; the liquid waters took up residence on earth while mist, fog, and cloud moisture took up residency in the atmosphere above the earth. The two connected to create a dense fog that extended from the heavens to the earth. This

7

combination of waters impeded the light from fully shining through to the earth; that prevented it from performing its life-producing functions. So once again God spoke, and His words went into action and separated the waters of the heavens from the waters of earth by a firmament He called the sky. The separating of the waters created another essential system which is essential for life, the weather and air.

One key function of the atmospheric heaven in God's plan was to provide life-sustaining water for the earth and its inhabitants. The waters on earth and in the atmosphere play a major role in providing food and sustainability for every living thing on earth. Water has many distinct properties critical for the acceleration of life in all creation. Water occupies approximately 70 percent of earth's space, and God's recycling process of water is a miracle. The functional value of water in God's creation makes it invaluable, as are all His systems. It is amazing how He had the systems work together to form functional, holistic structures. I encourage you to set aside time to study facts about water such as these from *Meriam-Webster's Dictionary*.

> "Seventy percent of the earth comprises water. Ninety-seven percent of the earth's water is in oceans and seas, while two percent is found on the icecaps. Enormous bodies of water can absorb and store large amounts of heat coming from the sun, especially during daytime and summer. Seventy-five percent of the human body is made up of water, and 90 percent of human blood is water."2

The air that surrounds the earth provides weather and life for all breathing things. We will discover later the role breathing plays in the spiritual and natural realms of God's creation story.

After speaking of the separation of the earthly and heavenly waters, God did not express His approval by stating that it was good as He had stated on day one. Does that have any ramifications?

We must not forget that God is a God of unity, so each system He spoke into existence was dependent on the other systems to create a unified, functional structure. In the first two days of creation, we have two major

systems created by God essential for fulfilling His de
and weather.

We must again point out that God had create
earth prior to His makeover. The word *heavens* is
existed. The first heaven was where God's kingdom
ruled—His heavenly kingdom. The second heaver
outer space, where the stars and moon exist to provide light to earth. The
third heaven is the atmospheric heaven where weather and air reside so life
can exist on earth.

Again, research this information and become as familiar as you can
with it. Your knowledge of God and His provisions will increase your faith
in God, and you will be a blessing to fellow brothers and sisters; plus, you
will enhance your relationship and fellowship with God.

Do you see your story aligning with God's creation story on day two?
What is your takeaway from day two?

> For the LORD is a great God, a great King above all gods.
> He holds in his hands the depths of the earth and the
> mightiest mountains. The sea belongs to him, for he made
> it. His hands formed the dry land, too. (Psalm 95:3–5)

2. *Merriam-Webster*, s.v. "app (*n.*)," accessed September 23, 2020,
http://www.merriam-webster.com/dictionary/app.

CHAPTER 3

Earth's Makeover

Then God said, "Let the waters beneath the sky flow together into one place, so dry ground may appear." And that is what happened. God called the dry ground "land" and the waters "seas." And God saw that it was good. Then God said, "Let the land sprout with vegetation— every sort of seed-bearing plant, and trees that grow seed-bearing fruit. These seeds will then produce the kinds of plants and trees from which they came." And that is what happened. The land produced vegetation—all sorts of seed-bearing plants, and trees with seed-bearing fruit. Their seeds produced plants and trees of the same kind. And God saw that it was good. And evening passed, and morning came, marking the third day. (Genesis 1:9–13)

The Third Day

God spoke forth the waters to flow together in one place so dry ground would appear. He added value to the ground and water by giving them personal names—land and seas—which reflected the value God placed on His systems. Their names in actuality define their assigned roles as we shall see.

God again extended His approval of the makeover of land and water by the resounding expression "And God saw that it was good." Again, we witness the creative powers of God as He strategically made geographical changes to what existed to create an organized and unified structure. He did not throw away anything—He just improves everything, which includes you. His master plan is an awesome example of interdependent systems united and working together. The Church is established upon those principles.

In Genesis 1:11, God continued His third day of creation.

> Then God said, "Let the land sprout with vegetation— every sort of seed-bearing plant, and trees that grow seed- bearing fruit. These seeds will then produce the kinds of plants and trees from which they came. And that is what happened."

God meticulously described how each system in His universal structure would function to produce His desired outcomes. God wonderfully input what was necessary to achieve the desired output. God created time on the first day and weather and air on the second day; on the third day, he created a third major system, food. God spoke His desire, and His word raced off to bring it into existence. He spoke His functional commands of continuous increase through ongoing fruitfulness and reproduction for plant life. What a powerful and majestic God, who has supreme wisdom to provide added value to His systems to keep them productive. Reproduction through the seeds by the various plants is essential in sustaining ongoing, like-kind life accomplished through sowing and reaping.

Genesis 1:12 highlights the functional purpose of the land: "The land produced vegetation—all sorts of seed-bearing plants, and trees with seed- bearing fruit. Their seeds produced plants and trees of the same kind." The functional response God desired once again came to fruition and was given His expression of approval: "And God saw that it was good."

Do you see your story aligning with God's creation story on day three? What is your takeaway from day three?

> You send rain on the mountains from your heavenly home, and you fill the earth with the fruit of your labor.

You cause grass to grow for the livestock and plants for people to use. You allow them to produce food from the earth—wine to make them glad, olive oil to soothe their skin, and bread to give them strength. They all depend on you to give them food as they need it. When you supply it, they gather it. You open your hand to feed them, and they are richly satisfied. (Psalm 104:13–15)

CHAPTER 4

Creation of the Stellar Heaven

Then God said, Let great lights appear in the sky to separate the day from the night. Let them mark off the seasons, days, and years. Let these lights in the sky shine down on the earth. And that is what happened. God made two great lights, the sun and the moon—the larger one to govern the day, and the smaller one to govern the night. He also made the stars. God set these lights in the sky to light the earth, to govern the day and night, and to separate the light from the darkness. And God saw that it was good. And evening passed and morning came, marking the fourth day. (Genesis 1:14–19)

Day Four

On day four, God expanded His light system He had spoken into existence on the first day. He identified the light as great lights and placed them in the sky. The once-waterlogged earth then comprised water, dry land, vegetation, seed-bearing trees, and plants. God provided the detailed functions of the lights so they would be known by their role in His unified design. They would separate the day from the night creating an identifiable time frame. God also used the lights to designate the seasons, days, and years that would further expand the time system of His unified structure. His creative time system is awesome; it displays essential functions by designated and visible sign sequences.

Time plays a major role in God's magnificent universe but especially on earth. His focus on time is intriguing. I consider it the cornerstone of existence and management oversight in contrast to the apostle Paul's identification of Jesus as the chief cornerstone of salvation in Ephesians 2:20–21.

> Together, we are his house, built on the foundation of the apostles and the prophets. And the cornerstone is Christ Jesus himself. We are carefully joined together in him, becoming a holy temple for the Lord.

The cornerstone is the focal point of the structure around it, and so is time. God used time to integrate all His structures so they would function interdependently to achieve His desired outcomes just as He made Jesus the cornerstone of His plan of salvation. Everything associated with God must flow through and align with Jesus, the only way of accessing God the Father. In John 14:6, Jesus said, "I am the way, the truth, and the life. No one can come to the Father except through me." This fundamental truth highlights God's line of communication; it is a management tool regulating order and decency in His kingdom displayed throughout all His creation.

In Genesis 1:13–14, God identified the functional roles of the great lights—the sun and moon—separated the day from the night, and marked off the seasons, days, and years. The scriptures also reveal that a day comprises three-time frames—morning, evening, and night. The scriptures show how God used functionality to shape time through visible demonstrations displayed by various defined characteristics. God's unified earthly structures required management intervention, which is essential for maintaining their created order (governance) and decency (character). For this to take place, God provided humankind with a major system to assist Him in governing the earth and everything inhabiting it—the interdependent system of time. Time is God's system of measurement for change in His unified structures. Ecclesiastes expresses this pointedly.

> For everything there is a season, a time for every activity under heaven. A time to be born and a time to die. A time to plant and a time to harvest. A time to kill and a time to heal. A time to tear down and a time to build up. A time to cry and a time to laugh. A time to grieve and a time to dance. A time to scatter stones and a time to gather stones. A time to embrace and a time to turn away. A time to search and a time to quit searching. A time to keep and a time to throw away. A time to tear and a time to mend. A time to be quiet and a time to speak. A time to love and a time to hate. A time for war and a time for peace. (Ecclesiastes 3:1–8)

Time causes major changes or transformations in every form of life. The changes are measurable by time frames, events, or identifiable and defined transformations. These time transformations are God's way of visibly communicating with His creation and causing His creation to react or respond in a designed way through transformational changes as recorded in Ecclesiastes 3:1–8 and throughout the Bible. We must understand the signs of the time so we can exist in harmony with God by knowing what divine actions we must take. In 1 Chronicles 12:32, we read, "From the tribe of Issachar, there were 200 leaders of the tribe with their relatives. All these men understood the signs of the times and knew the best course for Israel to take."

Let's continue exploring what God has in store for earth with all the interdependent systems in a unified structure. In Genesis 1:15, God commanded the lights to shine on earth, which highlighted His divine focus of attention. God desired certain outcomes for earth, and He created the essential inputs necessary for His desired outcomes to be achieved. I trust the creation story will cause you to embrace and know our majestic, Heavenly Father very personally. He is fabulous!

In Genesis 1:16–17, God continued to expand on the system of lights. He created two great lights and revealed their functions, the larger one to govern the day and the smaller one to govern the night. God added the glorious stars as another sign of His architectural grace. Again, God expressed His approval of the awesome light system that would play a major role in the time system as they worked together in His unified structure. The light system was assigned to govern day and night. It was out of His desire for order that He assigned functions of righteous governance to His systems. It is out of decency that He added moral value to His systems by assigning them spiritual and physical authority. Both work together to promote God's righteousness and holiness, His trademarks of perfection.

God did not command His systems to function without giving them His authority to execute them. He assigned authority throughout the ages as an added value of trust and responsibility to His multiple systems. Everything God created was good; however, after sin entered the world, everything became exposed to evil resulting in corruption, destruction and death.

God ended His fourth day as He had done previously: "And God saw that it was good."

Do you see your story aligning with God's creation story on day four? What is your takeaway from day four? What are your thoughts about sovereign authority?

> Praise him, sun and moon! Praise him, all you twinkling stars! Praise him, skies above! Praise him, vapors high above the clouds! Let every created thing give praise to the LORD, for he issued his command, and they came into being. He set them in place forever and ever. His decree will never be revoked. (Psalm 148:3–6)

CHAPTER 5

Creation of Sea Life and Birds

Then God said, "Let the waters swarm with fish and other life. Let the skies be filled with birds of every kind. So God created great sea creatures and every living thing that scurries and swarms in the water, and every sort of bird—each producing offspring of the same kind. And God saw that it was good. Then God blessed them, saying, "Be fruitful and multiply. Let the fish fill the seas, and let the birds multiply on the earth." And evening passed, and morning came, marking the fifth day. (Genesis 1:20–23)

Day Five

God's majesty of speaking creation into existence resumed on day five. He continued to expand the functional role of the waters, sky, and earth. The waters became home for various forms of sea life. The sky became the space for all birds. For the first time, God blessed His creatures, something He had not done previously; we can conclude that God's desire was for life to exist and reproduce and that He knew what that required—time, weather and air, and food. He created living creatures and in particular human beings to inhabit the earth and enjoy divine fellowship with Him. He demonstrated His divine power meticulously with His phenomenal makeover of earth and the cosmos for the benefit of its new inhabitants. He is awesome and worthy of praise!

God's blessing of the living creatures showed He held them in reverence and honor by speaking increase in production and fertility upon them. His blessing gave special recognition and honor to His life-producing creatures and sealed His functional relationship with them for His glory and their good. This is the precedent destined to be God's method of operation for all forms of life-producing creatures. God ended the fifth day as He did previously with His expression of approval, "And God saw that it was good."

Do you see your story aligning with God's creation story on day five? What is your takeaway from day five?

> Praise the LORD! Praise God in his sanctuary; praise him in his mighty heaven! Praise him for his mighty works; praise his unequaled greatness! Praise him with a blast of the ram's horn; praise him with the lyre and harp! Praise him with the tambourine and dancing; praise him with strings and flutes! Praise him with a clash of cymbals; praise him with loud clanging cymbals. Let everything that breathes sing praises to the LORD! Praise the LORD! (Psalm 150:1–6)

CHAPTER 6

Creation of the Animal Kingdom

Day Six A

> Then God said, "Let the earth produce every sort of animal, each producing offspring of the same kind—livestock, small animals that scurry along the ground, and wild animals." And that is what happened. God made all sorts of wild animals, livestock, and small animals, each able to produce offspring of the same kind. And God saw that it was good. (Genesis 1:24–25)

God expanded His creation of life by commanding the earth to produce every sort of animal and living creature. God assigned earth another functional role in His creation story; it was to produce animal life from the materials that composed it. He did not speak the animals into existence; instead, He authorized the earth to produce them. The earth is alive with many compositions from which life exists and was made from them. The earth and all non-soulish entities exist and consist of composite elements. When combined, they produce functional structural properties that work interdependently to fulfill God's desired outcome as a unified structural design. The created earth's composition materials exist to obey

God's command by producing various species of animal life. What an awesome demonstration of God's divine power transferred into His unified structure, earth, and its complementing systems. All of creation displays the value God places on unity by making every system interdependent or complementary of each other for maximum efficiency and effectiveness.

God's composition materials such as oxygen, silicon, aluminum, iron, calcium, sodium, potassium, magnesium, and other materials to make earth were taken from the earth to produce living creatures. I highly recommend researching scientific information about the elements and materials earth contains. It is fascinating to know that earth's composition is shared by all forms of life-producing creatures, including humans—magnificent! God maximized His systems and subsystems for a greater return through their interdependent functions.

God again incorporated His reproduction system into the animal kingdom. He made each species of animals to reproduce offspring of the same kind. God classified the animals as domesticated and wild; what an awesome creation strategy! We see the benefit of this decision played out in the relationship between domesticated animals and their masters and the food chain and ecosystem maintained and supplied by wild animals. God's design of the multiple functions required by each structure and the complementary value they transmitted to one another made their potential limitless in association with God, who is limitless.

The created structures responded to God's spoken commands as if they were living creatures. They might very well be because they respond to God's commands and comprise the same elements and minerals existing in all living creatures. Nothing for God was an afterthought; He masterfully planned the outcomes He desired based on order and decency. His truths or laws that exist in each system form interlocking procedures that make the systems operate flawlessly. When His truths are deviated from or changed, confusion with turmoil take over. Any opposition to God's norms becomes abnormal because its God-given function cannot be achieved. No one can change what God has established without suffering dire consequences from life to death.

After God made the different animal species, He ended as He did previously with His expression of approval, "And God saw that it was good."

Do you see your story aligning with God's creation story on day six A? What is your takeaway from day six A? Do you see the value in working with others?

> You alone are the LORD. You made the skies and the heavens and all the stars. You made the earth and the seas and everything in them. You preserve them all, and the angels of heaven worship you. (Nehemiah 9:6)

CHAPTER 7

Creation of Humanity

Day Six B

> Then God said, "Let us make human beings in our image, to be like ourselves. They will reign over the fish in the sea, the birds in the sky, the livestock, all the wild animals on the earth, and the small animals that scurry along the ground. (Genesis 1:26)

This glorious time in the creation story describes the creation of humankind, you and me. The previous five days of the creation story laid out God's creation of the universe with the focal point being the makeover of earth followed by the creation of vegetation and living creatures. The foundation of God's creation story is His desired outcome—a place where humanity would exist and cohabitate with Him in fellowship, so He designed a divine organized structure that would make that a reality. He wanted a personal relationship with His prized creation, humankind, and He wanted to exist in harmony with all His creation. Knowing that will allow our love, respect, and appreciation for God to become anchored in our souls.

The following verses will help us achieve a deeper appreciation of God and His organizational wisdom and make us strive to become His faithful and committed followers.

> The human body has many parts, but the many parts make up one whole body. So it is with the body of Christ. Some of us are Jews, some are Gentiles, some are slaves, and some are free. But we have all been baptized into one body by one Spirit, and we all share the same Spirit. Yes, the body has many different parts, not just one part. If the foot says, "I am not a part of the body because I am not a hand," that does not make it any less a part of the body. And if the ear says, "I am not part of the body because I am not an eye," would that make it any less a part of the body? If the whole body were an eye, how would you hear? Or if your whole body were an ear, how would you smell anything? But our bodies have many parts, and God has put each part just where he wants it. How strange a body would be if it had only one part! Yes, there are many parts, but only one body. The eye can never say to the hand, "I don't need you." The head can't say to the feet, "I don't need you." In fact, some parts of the body that seem weakest and least important are actually the most necessary. And the parts we regard as less honorable are those we clothe with the greatest care. So we carefully protect those parts that should not be seen, while the more honorable parts do not require this special care. So God has put the body together such that extra honor and care are given to those parts that have less dignity. This makes for harmony among the members, so that all the members care for each other. If one part suffers, all the parts suffer with it, and if one part is honored, all the parts are glad. All of you together are Christ's body, and each of you is a part of it. (1 Corinthians 12:12–27)

This speaks to the heart of God's creative strategy with the human body and His church—one body comprising many parts working interdependently together to achieve His desired outcomes as His unified structural whole. He created us to complement one another for the greater good of all as one which brings Him honor and glory. What an awesome God!

Let's return to the creation story in Genesis 1:26: "Then God said, 'Let us make human beings in our image, to be like ourselves.'" This is the beginning of human life as we know it. The scripture states, "let us make …" Genesis 1 provides us with a condensed version of the creation of human beings while Genesis 2 offers a detailed version of that. When He said, "Let us …" God was referring to Himself, His Son, Jesus Christ, and His Holy Spirit; the three are known as the Godhead, the heartbeat of the creation story.

God said, "make in our image and likeness …" An understanding of this statement is essential in getting to know God and our relationship to Him from the creation perspective. God did not include the words *image and likeness* when He created other living creatures. What about those words do we need to focus on?

It is important to know that you had nothing to do with you being you, it is all God; it was God who created you for His glory and honor. As a new child of God, I wanted to know Him better and draw closer to Him. One beautiful spring morning while praying in my basement, I wondered, *how can I know Him and know He exists?* He responded to my heart; He instructed me to go outside and told me, *Look up at the sky and its array of beauty*. I did, and He said, *That's me*. Then he said, *Look at the plants, trees, grass, and flowers*. I did, and He again said, *That's me*. He then instructed me, *Look at the birds and squirrels … That's me. Now look at your hands, your feet, your body … That's me.*

I wept deeply as I went back to my prayer room and praised Him. From that day forward, I had confident assurance that God was my awesome, Heavenly Father and that I could know Him through myself, one of His grateful children.

Image and likeness are not just physical but also spiritual matters. Humans are dualistic by creation, they are spirit and flesh, natural and spiritual independent systems that are united in the human structure. John 4:24 reads; "For God is Spirit, so those who worship him must worship in spirit and in truth." Colossians 1:5–17 describes the image of

God through the visible image of Christ, who took on flesh to represent humanity on behalf of God. The truths of the New Testament play a major role in helping us comprehend the truths of the Old Testament. As Bible scholars state, the New Testament is concealed in the Old Testament and the Old Testament is revealed in the New Testament. I hope this will help us understand the dichotomy of humankind at creation. *Stop*

God's key attribute, the foundation of all the others, is His genuine agape love as stated in 1 John 4:8: "But anyone who does not love does not know God, for God is love." God is the Spirit of love. It is out of His loving Spirit that He created human beings in His image and likeness so a loving, spiritual relationship would exist. He showed His love by providing the most precious resources for a quality life experience so humans could live in fellowship with Him.

God expresses His love in two areas: His righteousness and his holiness. Everything God created comprised His righteousness and holiness. These two truths govern every divine structure created by God for God. Functional fruitfulness and multiplication cannot happen without guidelines for governance and moral conduct. You will see His righteousness and holiness challenged throughout the ages from His human creation.

Verse 26 continues with the functional responsibilities of human beings after being created in God's image and likeness. He gave them the responsibility to reign over all other created beings and oversee their well-being to maintain order and decency on earth. All functions given by God come with sovereign authority so that assignments can be accomplished with His blessings. It reveals God's trust in humankind's relationship with Him through the sharing of oversight responsibilities.

God created human beings as male and female, essential for increase. Remember, God assigned a functional responsibility to every system He created. Human beings are defined by the functions God placed on them. God's reproductive system for human beings required males and females to fulfill the function of reproduction mandated by God.

In Genesis 1:28, we read, "God blessed the man and woman and commanded them to be fruitful and multiply. Fill the earth and govern it. Reign over the fish in the sea, the birds in the sky, and all the animals that scurry along the ground." God's blessing was a sign of His approval of His created vessels and the functions they would fulfill in His unified structure. He was affirming them so their confidence in His demonstrated grace would cause fruitful success in fulfilling their functional assignments. They were being tasked to reproduce offspring, to fill the earth with more humans, and to govern it by reigning over all living creatures. What an awesome assignment!

God does not give anyone more than he or she is able to bear. God designed everything to work together for His glory. His blessings assure us that we can accomplish His will for His glory and our good. God created and equipped us for outstanding productive and fruitful successes!

In verse 29, God said, "Look! I have given you every seed-bearing plant throughout the earth and all the fruit trees for your food." God supplied us with all we needed. His initial food menu for humans was vegetarian. It reveals God as Jehovah Jireh; He provided what we needed in our best interests for His glory and our good. God cared about every aspect of His new creation.

Time, weather and air, and food allow us to exist and govern earth. This implies that God created human beings with the intelligence to give oversight to His redesigned earth and its living inhabitants. God's rules, laws, or truths exist in each system and form a pattern of interlocking procedures that allows the systems to operate flawlessly by the governance of His righteousness and holiness.

Adam and Eve were governed by God's truths and commands. He had created them, so He knew everything about them. Only He could provide them the operational manual, His truths, to govern them. God added value to the man and woman by creating them in His image and likeness and giving them authority over the earth and its inhabitants based on His truths and commands.

Truth is God's directive in achieving His desired outcomes for the good of all. Obedience to God's truths always brings honor and glory to Him and success to humankind and their offspring. God shows His loving-kindness by always providing what we need to have victorious and joyous lives on earth. The governance functions God assigned to humankind were an awesome display of His goodness, generosity, and trust in them. He portrayed His trust by sharing His earthly kingdom with humankind and blessing them to function as managers of His redesigned earth and all living creatures.

He is selfless; He did not have to give humans free will to choose, but He did. His not withholding any good thing from His trophy creation reflected His graceful heart. God provided humans with intelligence, which equipped them to have an interactive relationship with the Godhead and fulfill the mandated functions over their new home, earth. Humans were created to be key players in the management of God's wonderful, new, earthly kingdom. Their assigned functions enabled them to work freely and in harmony with God and all the other living creatures.

The assignments given to humans showcase why God's nature of order and decency exists through His truths. Truth provides the framework of divine guidance humans need to fulfill their roles within their authority. Since humans were created in God's image and likeness, they function under God's governance and authority and are accountable to God based on their free will. We will see this played out later, but it is essential to note this now. Luke 12:24 tells us,

> But someone who does not know, and then does something wrong, will be punished only lightly. When someone has been given much, much will be required in return; and when someone has been entrusted with much, even more will be required.

Humans were getting ready to experience the righteousness and holiness of God's truths.

In Genesis 1:30, God extended His grace to His newly created humans by informing them, "Every green plant has been created as feed for all animal life." This is a clear witness of God's care for His creation and His commitment in His relationship with them. Providing food for the animals was His way of saying to humankind, "I am here to bless you with my support by easing your burden." What a mighty and good God!

Genesis 1:31 states, "Then God looked over all he had made, and he saw that it was very good! And evening passed and morning came, marking the sixth day." I can only imagine what God must have felt after six days of taking nothing and creating a complete makeover of earth to accommodate plant life, animal life, and human beings created in His blessed image and likeness. Verse 31 says it perfectly: "It was very good."

We need to study God's response here. Instead of "God saw that it was good," we read, "He saw that it was very good." *Very* implies extremely gratifying and pleasing. God was expressing His joy at seeing His whole structure functioning as He had designed it to.

Based on all I have been afforded to see and experience because of His great creation story, I am honored and privileged to agree with God. The story birthed new life eternally into my story, and I too can say it is very good. It is important for all to maximize their life story and secure their eternal reward by functioning under God's divine truths and laws of eternal life. Remember, God is the supreme authority over everything; He made everything for His honor and glory, and all living creatures benefit from His loving-kindness not to abuse it or ignore it but to love and live it!

Do you see your life story aligning with God's creation story, human beings, on day six B? What is your takeaway from day six B?

> You made all the delicate, inner parts of my body and knit me together in my mother's womb. Thank you for making me so wonderfully complex! Your workmanship is marvelous—how well I know it. You watched me as I was being formed in utter seclusion, as I was woven together in the dark of the womb. You saw me before I was born. Every day of my life was recorded in your book. Every moment was laid out before a single day had passed. How precious are your thoughts about me, O God. They cannot be numbered! I can't even count them; they outnumber the grains of sand! And when I wake up, you are still with me! (Psalm 139:13–18)

CHAPTER 8

The Day of Rest

Genesis chapter 2 will continue to present God's creation story, and how it shapes our life story.

> So the creation of the heavens and the earth and everything in them was completed. On the seventh day God had finished his work of creation, so he rested from all his work. And God blessed the seventh day and declared it holy, because it was the day when he rested from all his work of creation. (Genesis 2:1–4)

Day Seven

In verse 1, God's creation of the heavens and the earth was completed. He took six days to create the cosmos whereas He could have spoken everything into existence in one word or sentence instantly instead of taking six days. As we discussed, time is instrumental in all He does. However, the six days reveal His design and desired outcomes: His implementation of inputs, His use of time, His focus on the systems' interdependency, His trust of shared governance, His implementation of oversight, His preparation of reproductive systems, and His provision of the Sabbath Day of rest.

God carried out a seven-day sequence to teach humankind that His creation was a blueprint for humans to replicate. Human beings' architectural accomplishments throughout the ages support the idea that God's blueprints are still in use despite us. We must continue to avail ourselves of our Creator, who has given us everything pertaining to life and godliness, including the blueprints to manage it.

Humankind cannot create anything because everything needed to exist already exists—the elements, minerals, atmosphere, food, time, and so on. The reason God could exemplify joy and victory with His Son, Jesus, His Holy Spirit, and the angelic host by saying, "The creation of the heavens and the earth and everything in them were completed" (Genesis 2:1). God gave us the ability to invent, discover, and construct with His created resources.

Genesis 2:2 continues defining the days in a numerical sequence: "On the seventh day God finished his work of creation, so He rested from all his work." When you study the scientific makeup of the earth alone, you could easily assume it would take years and even centuries of construction with all its elements, minerals, etc. If that were not overwhelming enough, add the created, life-giving inhabitants on earth, and then add the two heavens, atmospheric and stellar, created to fulfill the functional outcome for life to exist on earth. When you envision all the systems that creation required, it is only realistic to say that we would never have completed such an undertaking.

He expressed His reward for accomplishing this creative miraculous work with these words: "He rested." *Strong's Concordance* identifies two words that defines "rested" that resonated with my spirit:—*... cease, celebrate...*[2]

Verse 3 expresses God's act of celebrating His rest after creating everything. He blessed the seventh day and declared it holy, worthy of His favor and approval. God sets aside what He blesses for His glory and honor. God's blessings are the highest and most cherished awards He grants. God's blessings elevate the recipients—people, places, or objects—to a level of divine honor and favor. Therefore, God's blessing of the seventh day was His act of consecrating the day back to Himself. He declared it a sacred day of reverence to Himself. Holiness denotes God's nature and

---

[2] Strong, J. 2009. *A Concise Dictionary of the Words in the Greek Testament and The Hebrew Bible* (vol. 2, 112). Bellingham, WA: Logos Bible Software.

character, which must be a preeminent reality for all humanity. Let's review some scriptures that will support this truth.

> The LORD also said to Moses, Give the following instructions to the entire community of Israel. You must be holy because I, the LORD your God, am holy. Each of you must show great respect for your mother and father, and you must always observe my Sabbath days of rest. I am the LORD your God. (Leviticus 19:1–3)

> So set yourselves apart to be holy, for I am the LORD your God. Keep all my decrees by putting them into practice, for I am the LORD who makes you holy. (Leviticus 20:7–8)

God is righteous and holy; those qualities are His nature, character, and attributes all wrapped together. It is the basis from which love, His most powerful expression, flows. His holiness results in His supernatural display of agape love. His order represents righteousness, and His decency represents His holiness; everything He created is righteous and holy by association with Him.

God's creation of life benefits from His glorious day of rest, a governance resource given by Him to humanity. It is a time to recuperate from laboring by fellowshipping with family and friends and reflecting on God while worshiping with others. All should bless what God blesses and deem holy what He deems holy. Children of God's way of life derives from Him, and we do what we see Father God doing. Everyone should have a consecrated Sabbath once a week. Your Sabbath will become an added asset to your health and life story with God and others.

Verse 4 concludes by affirming the previous verse, which provided a narrative of facts concerning God's creation of the heavens and the earth, which revealed His heart. God's nature of order and decency displays itself in His unified structural design in which every system has a function that complements all the others and creates extraordinary power.

Beyond the Godhead, the greatest asset to humanity is humanity. We must learn to cherish and value one another because we are God's gifts to one another. When we work for the good of others and esteem others more than we do ourselves, we all become blessings. Ecclesiastes 4:9–12 helps clarify this truth.

> Two people are better off than one, for they can help each other succeed. If one person falls, the other can reach out and help. But someone who falls alone is in real trouble. Likewise, two people lying close together can keep each other warm. But how can one be warm alone? A person standing alone can be attacked and defeated, but two can stand back-to-back and conquer. Three are even better, for a triple-braided cord is not easily broken.

To whom can you reach out and add value to, making them better together? Be a difference maker. Just live it!

God resolved to do things in a decent and orderly fashion so we would experience a healthy outcome. Decency denotes God's holiness, and order denotes His righteousness; those attributes combine to define His divine nature and character and result in His desired outcome. We see His holiness and righteousness throughout His creation narrative. Holiness and righteousness are divine expressions of the honor, dedication, and goodness of the Godhead and all associated with it through the simple act of loving obedience.

A loving passion for Father God motivates one to keep His commandments as an act of honor and respect. Everything associated with Him is righteous and holy. God assigned responsibilities to help His structures fulfill their purposes. Order and decency are organizing tools that govern individuals and organizations. God assigned governance oversight to the sun and moon as it relates to their respective functions— day and night lights. He also assigned governing responsibilities to human beings to reign over all living creatures and govern the earth and everything that inhabits it, including themselves. Those organizing responsibilities define the line of communication and accountability between God and humankind. Righteousness and holiness are the likeness of God, and they were foundational in His creation of humankind so unity in accomplishing

His divine relational outcome would become a reality. Let's continue to see where the narrative takes us.

Do you see your story aligning with God's creation story on day seven? Have you designated a day of rest? What is your takeaway from day seven?

> For the word of the LORD holds true, and we can trust everything he does. He loves whatever is just and good; the unfailing love of the LORD fills the earth. The LORD merely spoke, and the heavens were created. He breathed the word, and all the stars were born. He assigned the sea its boundaries and locked the oceans in vast reservoirs. Let the whole world fear the LORD, and let everyone stand in awe of him. For when he spoke, the world began! It appeared at his command. (Psalm 33:4–9)

CHAPTER 9

Detailed Account of Earth's Makeover

> This is the account of the creation of the heavens and the earth. When the LORD God made the earth and the heavens, neither wild plants nor grains were growing on the earth. The LORD God had not yet sent rain to water the earth, and there were no people to cultivate the soil. Instead, springs came up from the ground and watered all the land. (Genesis 2:4–6)

This is the detailed account of God's creation story. Genesis 1 was a *Reader's Digest* version of it that highlighted and gave a basic overview of creation. The detailed account will give us some key information about creation that will help us fall deeper in love with our awesome Heavenly Father and help us appreciate our life story.

It is fascinating to see God continue His creative work this time as a landscape designer. Verse 5 gives us an overview of what existed on earth prior to the creation of man. There was no plant life on earth prior to its makeover because God had not provided it with water or people to manage it. God allowed water to come up from underground to water the land; I think an unknown dysfunction apparently flooded the land. We can surmise this based on Genesis 1:1, where deep water is said to have covered the land.

It is apparent that God, prior to His makeover of earth and modern humans, created the earth at a future time. The only source of earth's prehistoric time biblically is recorded in Genesis 2:4 (KJV): "These *are* the generations of the heavens and of the earth when they were created, in the day that the LORD God made the earth and the heavens." Remember, the earth and water existed prior to God's supernatural makeover; the earth and heavens existed for generations prior to God's makeover.

Geology provides some guidance here. Geologists have estimated the earth to be approximately 4.5 billion years old. I know there has been a divide between science and religion over creation. I will be the first to say that scientific theories addressing the origin of life on earth such as the big bang theory, the one-cell animal theory, the electric spark theory, and the outer-space theory among others are false. They have one purpose in mind—to deny God.

The biblical account of God and creation is the only truthful description of the existence of the earth and all that dwells on it. I came to that conclusion due to God's desire to create human beings for His honor and glory. None of those theories has a definitive, desired-outcome purpose that would justify their reason for being. Things just do not happen; they are ordered! Creation is a divine masterpiece that portrays God as the Creator of everything coexisting in love and unity for the good of all. Creation was not an accident that just happened; it exists and functions as its Creator God ordered it to. Life is order and decency—it never just happens—it must be contended for. Those theories do not meet that criteria. I am a supporter of "good" science and its positive accomplishments. Good science is a gift from God to humankind and earth as long as it does not demean God. Anything and anyone who dismisses God's existence or attempts to destroy His creation are anti-God and are operating in error and in need of God's grace.

When science studies the earth and its dwellers for the good of all, I see that as a gift from God. When science works for their destruction rather than for their good, I see that as an act of evil, which we will address later. Since good science is associated with God's creation, the results of archeological studies can help us appreciate God more because His accomplishments throughout the ages are based on His truths.

I agree with science that the generations of the heavens and the earth are equivalent to approximately 4.5 billion years. We can only imagine what God created and what took place during that time, but that should not be the dominant reason we pursue God. We pursue God because of His majestic love for all humanity and the promised future, eternal life He has guaranteed us. He will liberate us from the curse of death and the evils of Satan so that we will be with him forever in our new, glorified bodies. Our promised future should highlight our brief life on a judged world and its earthly systems (the Lake of Fire). Do not allow yourself to be deceived into believing there is something better than what God has planned for your precious life, which He purchased through His Son, Jesus—There isn't!

Genesis 1:5–6, 9 describes to us what the earth looked like prior to God's makeover. This narrative gives more details of why day three of creation was so essential. God provided reservoirs for the water to settle in leaving sections of dry land. The water was the source of life for all vegetation on the land. God had not released rain from the sky at that point. He wanted dry land to be able to produce food for humans and animals. Don't you just love God? He's super!

Can you see your life story aligning with the earth? What are your thoughts about the prehistoric existence of the earth and possible inhabitants? What is your view of an ordered life that reflects God's righteousness and holiness?

CHAPTER 10

The Human Structure—The Spirit System

Genesis 2:7 gives clarity to God's most cherished creation—humans. Genesis 1:27 states, "So God created human beings in his own image. In the image of God he created them; male and female, he created them." This is an abbreviated narrative of God's creation of human beings; however, it is very essential to grasp this truth so that the relationship God desires with humankind will come to fruition.

Previously, we dealt with the dualistic—spiritual and natural—nature of humankind. Being created in God's image means possessing His righteousness and holiness, which are birthed in the spiritual realm and manifested in the physical realm. In John 4:24, Jesus said, "God *is* a Spirit: and they that worship him must worship *him* in spirit and in truth." This profound truth infers that God created man with a spirit so humankind could function in a divine relationship with the Godhead during their earthly existence.

We need to understand human life from God's perspective because it provides the only means for living orderly and decent lives that will honor and glorify Him and reward His obedient children with eternal life. The Bible highlights five words (subsystems) that describe the spiritual system of humankind—spirit, heart, mind, body, and soul. We will discuss each to reveal how God aligned His creation to be in harmony with Him. The spiritual and the natural aspects of human beings have many subsystems identified by their independent functions designed to work interdependently to form a unified structure known as human beings.

Concerning the soul of man, Ecclesiastes 12:7 (KJV) states, "Then shall the dust return to the earth as it was: and the spirit shall return unto God who gave it." This verse will help us understand that the soul of man is like a pendulum hanging between the poles of the natural body and the spirit body. It will always gravitate toward the body, which controls it. The natural and spiritual bodies war against one another for control of the soul of man. Mark 14:38 (KJV) reads, "Watch ye and pray, lest ye enter into temptation. The spirit truly *is* ready, but the flesh *is* weak." We must value our souls and guard them lest they spend eternity in the Lake of Fire.

Let's start with identifying the functional purpose of the spirit system first and explore what the Holy Spirit gave us through the Word. The apostle Paul in 1 Corinthians 2:11–16 (KJV) wrote,

> For what man knoweth the things of a man, save the spirit of man which is in him? even so the things of God knoweth no man, but the Spirit of God. Now we have received, not the spirit of the world, but the spirit which is of God; that we might know the things that are freely given to us of God. Which things also we speak, not in the words which man's wisdom teacheth, but which the Holy Ghost teacheth: comparing spiritual things with spiritual. But the natural man receiveth not the things of the Spirit of God: for they are foolishness unto him: neither can he know *them*, because they are spiritually discerned. But he that is spiritual judgeth all things, yet he himself is judged of no man. For who hath known the mind of the Lord, that he may instruct him? But we have the mind of Christ.

The Word confirms that humans have a spirit in them and that God is a Spirit and has a Spirit. It establishes that only the spirit of a person knows the thoughts of the person and that only God's Spirit knows His thoughts. He continues to present us with the functions of the spirit of man and the Spirit of God as the key sources of communication between God and humankind.

We have learned from God how essential communication—the conveying of knowledge and information about someone or something to another—is to human existence. God, a Spirit, created humankind with a spirit so they could commune. God's communication system exists to make known the things He has freely given us to possess through His truths. Without the knowledge of His truths, we would not be able to communicate intelligently with Him concerning our needs and requests and His will for us.

Knowledge is power; its absence would prevent us from receiving what God has provided us resulting in dysfunctional behavior. Communing with God is the only way to know Him, His ways, His thoughts, and His will and be in harmony with Him. When we live in harmony with God, we honor and glorify Him, and He responds by granting His favor on His faithful ones. He wants a righteous and holy relationship with us. His input required creating humans with spirits so their identity would align with His. Without a spirit, humankind could not exist in harmony with God. Zechariah 12:1 (KJV) tells us, "The burden of the word of the LORD for Israel, saith the LORD, which stretcheth forth the heavens, and layeth the foundation of the earth, and formeth the spirit of man within him."

God formed the spirit in human beings for His benefit and humanity's good—this truth is supported by Job 32:8: "But there is a spirit within people, the breath of the Almighty within them, that makes them intelligent."

As we explore God's creation of humankind from the spiritual, invisible realm, we must look at the first subsystem, the soul of humans. Genesis 2:7 (KJV) introduces the word *soul* to us: "And the LORD God formed man *of* the dust of the ground and breathed into his nostrils the breath of life; and man became a living soul." God formed man from the ground He had created in a previous age that reappeared when He sent the waters to reservoirs. God made man a physical body from the dust of the earth to house his spiritual system made in the likeness of the Godhead. (We will discuss the physical body later.) God then breathed life into that body, and man became a living soul. God imparted Himself into humankind when He breathed into him, a clear indicator of His love for humankind.

Man thus became a functional being with a body and spirit fit for His divine purpose. Isaiah 43:7 (KJV) states, "*Even* every one that is called by my name: for I have created him for my glory, I have formed him; yea, I have made him."

We were made in God's image and likeness; we are one with Him for His glory and honor and can worship Him in harmony with His righteousness and holiness imparted to us by His Spirit. The result is true worship of God that can be accomplished only by living in accordance with God's truths through a spirit anointed and born again by the indwelling of the Holy Spirit. The power to transform our lives into the image of God's divine nature and character is what defines us as true worshipers. Worshipping is living as Jesus did, and praising is the verbal expression of our thanks to Him for His loving-kindness. Job 33:4 expands on this truth: "For the Spirit of God has made me, and the breath of the Almighty gives me life."

A living soul in a body can achieve the outcome God designated for His glory. In Genesis 2:5, His human structure would manage His earth by cultivating the soil from which he had been created. The earth benefits from the management oversight of humankind for preservation, and humankind benefits from earth's provisions to sustain human life. God designed humankind and the earth to complement each other. The decency and order of God's creative mind demands a response of "Awesome!"

Let us look at the functional responsibility of the soul of man. "The soul is the life of a man, the consciousness, the breath, the essence, the being of a man. The seat of man's breath and life or consciousness" and "the immaterial, invisible part of man" (*Practical Word Study New Testament* and *Vine's Complete Expository Dictionary*). The most practical description of the soul is in Genesis 2:7: "And man became a living person." God formed the body from the dust, but it was without the ability to function; it needed life to flow through it to become functional. The human structure would consist of the spirit system and natural system all dressed up but with no place to go without life, like a mannequin with no means to exist.

To assure His desired outcome, God breathed life into the body, and it became a living soul. There was no power to operate man until God breathed into his nostrils. There is nothing man has done or can do to produce life because God is the only source of life. The human structure permits the interchangeable use of terms such as *soul, man, person, being, heart,* and *body.* Our souls are the living us composed of our natural and spiritual systems. The only way we can appreciate ourselves and others is through the eyes of the Lord God by knowing why He made us—to be in fellowship with Him and one another.

Do you see your life story aligning with God's creation story? What is your takeaway from Genesis 2:5–7?

The second spirit subsystem is the heart, our center, our most vital part. It determines what we do and how we behave; we define ourselves by our moral or immoral conduct. The heart is the source of a person's rational or irrational behaviors manifested through reasoning, understanding, thinking, and imagining either good or evil. Our hearts establish the intellectual guidance we need to live decent and orderly lives.

God did not create human beings to control them but to choose Him as their heavenly Father of their free will. The heart is the communication link between the Lord God and humanity that signals the state of a person's heart. The heart's condition of being will signal which system—spiritual or natural—is managing it, and what—good or evil—is coming out of it.

Our hearts are central in fulfilling the purpose the Lord God has for us; they are central to the thoughts and imaginations generated by the spirit or natural body that translate into behaviors or actions either good or evil. Our free will allows us to choose which system will control our lives. Our hearts keep us in step with God or out of step with Him. Free will is a valued treasure if we use it to follow Jesus and receive eternal life, escaping eternal damnation.

Let a pure and grateful heart shape your free-will choice for good. The Holy Spirit is waiting for you to receive Him as your personal confidant to lead you into all truth and righteousness so your free choices will always honor God, who is your life.

Luke 6:45 reveals how good or evil begins in the heart and starts with thoughts and imaginations in the mind: "A good person produces good things from the treasury of a good heart, and an evil person produces evil things from the treasury of an evil heart. What you say flows from what is in your heart." Matthew 9:4 reads, "Jesus knew what they were thinking, so he asked them, 'Why do you have such evil thoughts in your hearts?'" And Genesis 6:5 (KJV) reads, "And GOD saw that the wickedness of man *was* great in the earth, and *that* every imagination of the thoughts of his heart *was* only evil continually."

God monitors the heart of every human. The heart is His computer that conveys the status of one's true self whether good or evil. It is also God's gift to humanity so we can monitor our lives. The heart is the scorecard that will determine our future abode. Our lifestyles are outward displays of what is in our hearts, who we really are. The key function of the heart is to help us maintain alignment with God's heart and live in a way that honors and glorifies Him.

Do all you can to keep your heart righteous and holy because it is the line of communication God uses to order your life for good. Your heart is a major asset, and if you monitor it with God's truths and convictions, you will always quench the fiery attempts of evil and live a righteous and holy life. Lying deceptions are the foundations on which evil is birthed in the hearts of humanity.

Do you see your life story aligning with God's creation story? What is your takeaway from the study of the heart? Are your free-will choices revealing the state of your heart to you? Monitor your heart continuously!

> For the weapons of our warfare are not carnal but mighty in God for pulling down strongholds, casting down arguments and every high thing that exalts itself against the knowledge of God, bringing every thought into captivity to the obedience of Christ. (2 Corinthians 10:4–5 NKJV)

The third spirit subsystem is the mind, which in some cases is synonymous with the heart. This is the last subsystem of the spirit system. From the mind flows thoughts, reasoning, understanding, intention, purpose, and attitude. God has given us intellectual powers; we were created to think, reason, and understand. A child of God's mind and thoughts should be centered on God. We are to love God with all our mind.

The mind is the processing subsystem of the spirit system. The mind compiles information from visual observations, physical interactions, reactions of the flesh, the environment, negative or positive circumstances, and good or bad life experiences. These perceptions from various sources are processed and dispersed to the heart, where the system in control will respond accordingly. This is a very important truth to comprehend. The heart is classified as good or evil based on the system in control—the natural/carnal flesh or the spiritual/righteous spirit. God aligns with the spirit rather than with the flesh of humans. The mind processes the information based on the system of source. It then transports the information through the central nervous subsystem, the brain, to be acted upon by the body. The behavior will identify the prevailing system whether good or evil.

> The sinful nature wants to do evil, which is just the opposite of what the Spirit wants. And the Spirit gives us desires that are the opposite of what the sinful nature desires. These two forces are constantly fighting each other, so you are not free to carry out your good intentions. (Galatians 5:17)

> When you follow the desires of your sinful nature, the results are very clear: sexual immorality, impurity, lustful pleasures, idolatry, sorcery, hostility, quarreling, jealousy, outbursts of anger, selfish ambition, dissension, division, envy, drunkenness, wild parties, and other sins like these. Let me tell you again, as I have before, that anyone living that sort of life will not inherit the Kingdom of God. But the Holy Spirit produces this kind of fruit in our lives: love, joy, peace, patience, kindness, goodness, faithfulness, gentleness, and self-control. There is no law against these things! (Galatians 5:19–23)

These verses along with many others help us know God and His purpose for creating us—to serve Him and others through our spirit beings, and that requires our subjecting our natural system to our spirit system. We will discuss later how God's very good human structure became a very evil human structure and created discord between the natural and spiritual systems.

We have completed our overview of the spirit system and the subsystems it comprises. Those subsystems are the operational components working interdependently making the system a functional part of the holistic structure.

Do you see your life story aligning with God's creation story? What is your takeaway from the study of the mind? What is your understanding of your spirit system, which comprises the soul, heart, and mind?

CHAPTER 11

The Human Structure—The Natural System

The body is the system God made from dust; it is the visible system of human beings that houses the spirit system. The uniqueness of the human system aligns with God's creative design of the cosmos and earth. They represent the order and decency of God's unified structures working as a whole. God's outcome defines His input. God's desire for a living being He could have a personal relationship with, manage His earth and all the inhabitants thereof, and be fruitful and multiply resulted in a finished structure called human beings.

Isaiah 45:18 states, "For the LORD is God, and he created the heavens and earth and put everything in place. He made the world to be lived in, not to be a place of empty chaos. 'I am the LORD,' he says, 'and there is no other.'"

God defines His systems by their functions. Humans were created to perform His spiritual and natural mandates. The two systems, one visible and one invisible, were created to work interdependently as fearfully and wonderfully made human structures. Psalm 139:13–16 reads,

> You made all the delicate, inner parts of my body and
> knit me together in my mother's womb. Thank you for

making me so wonderfully complex! Your workmanship is marvelous—how well I know it. You watched me as I was being formed in utter seclusion, as I was woven together in the dark of the womb. You saw me before I was born. Every day of my life was recorded in your book. Every moment was laid out before a single day had passed.

Awesome! Study the anatomy of your awesome body and discover how much God invested in you to be like Him. Focus on the purposes God assigned to humans so you can appreciate who you are. You are important, you are significant, and you are a blessing. God imparted Himself into you when He breathed life into you for His glory and honor.

He gave internal and external subsystems such as organs and limbs connected by bones, skin, ligaments, tendons, muscles, cells, atoms, and so on. He gave us fingers to touch Him, eyes to see Him, ears to hear Him, and a heart to pump blood and sustain our lives. Who could not love a God like Him? I fall in love with Him over and over when I look at myself—fearfully and wonderfully made for God by God. I love you, my heavenly Father, for investing in me!

Humankind as designed by God is finished. The human structure has the systems and subsystems that work as a whole to the perfect will of God. We are unique in that God gave us the freedom to reason and make choices, which demonstrates that He trusts us.

Do you see the value of your life story based on God's creation story? What is your takeaway from the way God created you?

CHAPTER 12

Planting the Garden of Eden

Let's study the beautiful environment God prepared for Adam and Eve to call home.

> Then the LORD God planted a garden in Eden in the east, and there he placed the man he had made. The LORD God made all sorts of trees grow up from the ground—trees that were beautiful and that produced delicious fruit. In the middle of the garden he placed the tree of life and the tree of the knowledge of good and evil. A river watered the garden and then flowed out of Eden and divided into four branches. The first branch, called the Pishon, flowed around the entire land of Havilah, where gold is found. The gold of that land is exceptionally pure; aromatic resin and onyx stone are also found there. The second branch, called the Gihon, flowed around the entire land of Cush. The third branch, called the Tigris, flowed east of the land of Asshur. The fourth branch is called the Euphrates. (Genesis 2:8–14)

God perfected organizing by designing the systems to complement one another and work together to achieve His desired outcomes. His wisdom was displayed in His making sure that no one system was superior to the other. Each system would be valueless if it were not a part of the whole, and the entire structure would be dysfunctional preventing the desired outcomes from fulfillment. God made sure that every system was maintained through sound management by adding value to each system through its independent functions that can operate only in harmony with each other. He also added resources to the systems to keep them functioning. Management is a form of refueling that supports and stimulates the systems so they can remain functional as a unified structure.

God added and directed the replication of each living system. Replication assures that the structures will be fruitful and multiply. God's demonstration of replication is manifested through His creation of humans in His image and likeness. It is also present through His reproduction system. Jesus reinforced that by instructing His disciples to follow Him and saying He would replicate himself through them so they could imitate His character and nature.

We can add value to others by helping them see themselves as children of God. We can resource ourselves by allowing the Holy Spirit to become our main confidant through positive initiatives in alignment with God's truths. We can become righteous and holy mentors by equipping others through giving ourselves away. We can replicate ourselves by pouring ourselves into others by valuing their souls.

Imitate Jesus, and desire to be one with God through Him with a divine compassion for those who are perishing. True management begins with managing yourself as a child of God by following Jesus so others will follow you.

Genesis 2:8–14 helps us understand God's investment in the creation of the garden of Eden. Note its meticulous details. The soil, the dust that God used to create humanity, also nourished the plants there. The trees were beautiful producers of delicious fruit. This gives us another example of how God's structures work interdependently to produce His desired outcomes.

God placed the tree of life and the tree of the knowledge of good and evil in the center of the garden because they would play a major role in His creation story. These two trees portrayed God's divine intention, to test the hearts of humankind. The center of any garden is usually the high-profile location that becomes the centerpiece of attraction and attention. The garden trees were beautiful and producers of delicious fruits. They were pleasant to see and good for food. In Genesis 2:9, God did not provide a stated purpose for the trees, just their names and location. God's creation scheme used names to define the function of His created structures. We can conclude that the Tree of Life was the source of everlasting life and that the Tree of the Knowledge of Good and Evil was the source of death. This conclusion is based on God's warning to Adam as stated in Genesis 2:16–17 and God's statement about life in Genesis 3:22.

The Tree of the Knowledge of Good and Evil is most interesting because it gives the impression of an oxymoron. The word *knowledge* means to have understanding of, insight to, information of, cognizance of, which implies, "I got this." Simply stated, knowledge means having the awareness of how something will impact your life if you choose to partake or engage in it. The word *good* means honorable, right, excellent, pleasing of the highest quality. Good is the nature and character of God. Good promotes life. The word *evil* denotes all the attributes of wickedness, which oppose the attributes of good. Evil means to be anti-God by attacking all that is good. Evil is the nature and character of Satan. Evil promotes sin which results in death. God placed those two trees strategically to test man's free-will choice of life or death. Man's choice of one of the two trees would determine the future of humankind—life or death. The catastrophe in the garden could have very well been the joy in the garden.

In Genesis 2:10–14, we learn that the garden's major source of water was a river that flowed through it. Water is the life-sustaining liquid, a valued treasure God created for all living matter. The river and its branches, the Pishon, the Gihon, the Tigris, and the Euphrates, flowed through various countries. I enjoy the beauty of various national parks, so I know that the garden of Eden would have blown my mind!

This is further evidence of God's love and added value for His human creation providing it with the best resources to assure productive and successful lives. Note the acknowledgement of the gold and precious stones that the ground contained; what a witness of the Lord God and His greatness shown by His ingenuity. God does not make junk, nor does He represent mediocrity, chaos, or indecency. He is our Heavenly Father from whom everything good flows.

In the garden, humankind and God fellowshipped in the cool of the day and discussed how to maintain order there. The only thing missing is God's approval response, "And God saw that it was good" (Genesis 1:10). Why? Think about it in terms of what would take place in the future.

Do you see your life story aligning with God's creation story? What is your takeaway from the way God created the garden of Eden for humankind?

After the garden of Eden was completed, God placed man in it.

> The LORD God placed the man in the Garden of Eden to tend and watch over it. But the LORD God warned him, "You may freely eat the fruit of every tree in the garden— except the tree of the knowledge of good and evil. If you eat its fruit, you are sure to die." (Genesis 2:15–17)

God revealed that all living things, including man, had to be organized and managed according to His purpose for each. His wisdom is displayed through implementing His system of checks and balances that assures functions are carried out as intended.

Man was placed in the garden of Eden to "tend and watch over it." Genesis 2:5 states, "There were no people to cultivate the soil"; God added value to man by assigning him oversight responsibilities. This insight is a profound teaching of God's strategic planning in directing the actions of humankind through organizing based on mission and purpose. Organizing is the directing and unifying of people, places, and objects for organizational success. Organizing defines the governance guidelines for maintaining order and the conduct required. Management serves as an interdependent control system to assure the systems and structures are functioning as designed. The desired outcomes must become the motivational forces for maintaining order and the appropriate moral conduct.

God was the creator and the chief executive officer of the cosmos and everything inhabiting it. The Godhead is the governing arm of all creation including Adam and Eve. God trusted them to do what was right and holy by providing him with instructions. Authority represents the power to establish lines of communications and the guidelines of accountability. In Genesis 3:16–17, God told man, "You may freely eat the fruit of every tree in the garden—except the tree of the knowledge of good and evil.

If you eat of its fruit, you are sure to die." This was the most significant communication between God and Adam. God created man with a free will; he could obey or disobey God's instructions. God instructed man to enjoy the fruit from all the trees in the garden but warned him not to eat the fruit from the one tree of the knowledge of good and evil. There were no subsequent recorded discussions about the tree between God and Adam until after Adam and Eve violated the warning, which leads to human speculation. I am sure in time, God and Adam discussed the warning again and in particular after Eve was created.

Do you see your life story aligning with God's creation story? What is your takeaway from the warning of God to Adam? What is your assessment of free will?

CHAPTER 13

The Creation of Woman

Then the LORD God said, "It is not good for the man to be alone. I will make a helper who is just right for him. So the LORD God formed from the ground all the wild animals and all the birds of the sky. He brought them to the man to see what he would call them, and the man chose a name for each one. He gave names to all the livestock, all the birds of the sky, and all the wild animals. But still there was no helper just right for him. So the LORD God caused the man to fall into a deep sleep. While the man slept, the LORD God took out one of the man's ribs and closed up the opening. Then the LORD God made a woman from the rib, and he brought her to the man. "At last!" the man exclaimed. "This one is bone from my bone, and flesh from my flesh! She will be called 'woman,' because she was taken from 'man.'" This explains why a man leaves his father and mother and is joined to his wife, and the two are united into one. Now the man and his wife were both naked, but they felt no shame. (Genesis 2:18–25)

God thus provided His strategic plan for humankind with a detailed description of His creation of the woman. The condensed version was provided in Genesis 1:27. God created man first and had an ongoing relationship with him prior to the creation of woman. The time that elapsed between the creation of man and woman is unknown; it is another opportunity for speculations. God's plan for man included woman so humans could reproduce. She would become man's intimate companion, helper, and reproduction soulmate. She was the missing link to complete God's functional structure of humankind. God was going to make a helper who was right for man.

Let us hold on for a minute because Genesis 2:19 and 20 just slipped in. There was more work to be completed by man before his helpmate would arrive. These verses reveal that after the creation of the animal kingdom, God gave man the responsibility of managing all living creatures. I am convinced that during the time man spent with God, he obeyed God resulting in God's approval and trust of him. God presented the animals to man to name, and he did so. As recorded in verse 20, a helper just right for him had not been provided. I am convinced that man's faithfulness to God made God aware of his needs. Faithfulness is the pathway to God's heart; it causes Him to act on behalf of His obedient ones. Could God have been testing man's patience? Think about it.

Genesis 2:21–22 returns to God's creative mode of making a woman for man. Here, God took on the role of a surgeon: "He causes man to fall into a deep sleep and while man is asleep; The Lord open up his body and removed one of man's ribs and closed it back up" to make "a helper just right for him." What an ingenious Father we have; He is aware of our needs and knows how to meet them. He could have made woman the same way He had made man, but the ways of the master architect are worth finding out; He made woman from a rib of man, and He presented her to the man. She is indeed a helper just right for him because she is in essence him in her and her in him; they are one flesh.

"At last!" the man exclaimed when he saw her. He was saying that his patience had paid a great reward. Isaiah 40:31 states, "But they that wait upon the Lord shall renew their strength; they shall mount up with wings as eagles; they shall run, and not be weary; and they shall walk, and not faint." The man's endurance brought his desired outcome. We must learn from our first dad's experiences with God so we can know Him and His ways; He changes not. Waiting on the Lord builds up our patience, which will be rewarded. Romans 15:4 (KJV) states, "For whatsoever things were written aforetime were written for our learning, that we through patience and comfort of the scriptures might have hope." Hope is a powerful motivator to keep us patiently waiting; our Heavenly Father will fulfill what He promised.

Man's joyous exclamation was compelling evidence that he had been discipled by God. His remarks were resounding with truth as he stated in Genesis 2:23 that she was "bone from my bone and flesh from my flesh!" He called her "woman, because she was taken from man." His response of this God created moment echoed down through ages as supported in Genesis 2:24: "This explains why a man leaves his father and mother and is joined to his wife, and the two are united into one." These words have been repeated at weddings attesting to this great institution of God, holy matrimony, the joining of a man and woman in marriage, which fulfills one purpose for which humans were created. Genesis 1:28 (KJV) states,

> And God blessed them, and God said unto them, Be fruitful, and multiply, and replenish the earth, and subdue it: and have dominion over the fish of the sea, and over the fowl of the air, and over every living thing that moveth upon the earth.

He was instructing them to be each other's helpmate, to have an intimate relationship, to reproduce, and to manage the earth and all living things on it. God personally communicated His functional purpose to man and woman together, and their assignments mandated accountability. God wanted them to succeed in their assignments. Obedience to God honors and worships Him, which must be the desire of every child of God.

I can only imagine their joy and happiness in paradise, where they had a personal audience with the Lord God. I can see myself fulfilling my responsibilities, fellowshipping with the animals, and exploring God's showcase of beauty. I would look forward to walking with God and listening to Him share His strategic plan for all creation. Having my helpmate to share all of God's glory within His presence and without a care in the world sounds like heaven to me. I can only imagine what it will be like to live eternally in the new paradise with my many love ones, brothers and sisters, and the Godhead.

What are your thoughts and imaginations about the creation of woman?

Genesis 2:25 tells us, "Now the man and his wife were both naked, but they felt no shame," and that ended the creation story. There has to be something God desired to impart at this point, so let's explore it and see what God revealed.

The mention of their nakedness is strange since they had always been naked; that must have been the dress code. They had been created pure and complete and without any cares or needs. Matthew 6:28–29 explain what I am implying: "And why worry about your clothing? Look at the lilies of the field and how they grow. They don't work or make their clothing; yet Solomon in all his glory was not dressed as beautifully as they are."

Man and woman existed in a state of innocence where no sin or evil existed, at least not then; their nakedness was not a concern because they knew nothing else. Since there was no law to judge their actions or behavior, there could be no sin producing shame or embarrassment. The apostle Paul wrote in Romans 3:20, "For no one can ever be made right with God by doing what the law commands. The law simply shows us how sinful we are." Romans 4:15 reads, "For the law always brings punishment on those who try to obey it. (The only way to avoid breaking the law is to have no law to break!)" Therefore, the verse is a precursor to what is about to come, the opposite of what was. The only thing close to a law would be the command with the dire consequence of death God gave the man in Genesis 2:16–17: "But the LORD God warned him, 'You may freely eat the fruit of every tree in the garden—except the tree of the knowledge of good and evil. If you eat its fruit, you are sure to die.'" I conclude that these verses were placed in a unique location to prepare us for the travesty to come. While writing, I got a very deep emotional steering in my spirit over Genesis 2:25. God's creation of woman was the final piece of the creation story. And then verse 25. It felt like a setup to steal my joy, just expressing myself. God knows how to get our attention.

Do you see your life story aligning with God's creation story? What is your takeaway from verse 25?

CHAPTER 14

The Fall of Humanity

Since verse 25 gave us a glimpse of what is coming, let's journey into Genesis 3, the basis of what would become humankind's fatal catastrophe.

The serpent was the shrewdest of all the wild animals the Lord God had made. One day, he asked the woman,

> "Did God really say you must not eat the fruit from any of the trees in the garden?" "Of course we may eat fruit from the trees in the garden," the woman replied. "It's only the fruit from the tree in the middle of the garden that we are not allowed to eat. God said, 'You must not eat it or even touch it; if you do, you will die.'" "You won't die!" the serpent replied to the woman. "God knows that your eyes will be opened as soon as you eat it, and you will be like God, knowing both good and evil." (Genesis 3:1–5)

This conversation is the most vicious in the history of humankind because of the catastrophic consequences that resulted from it and the evil pattern it established: "Just lie." We learn that the serpent was the crafty and cunning schemer of all the animals God had made. Did God give the animal kingdom free will also? The serpent was a schemer. Does that indicate he had free will? Could it speak the same language as humans? Was it capable of sinning?

Zollie L. Smith

Everything God created was good. Animals are soulish, living creatures. There had been no reported sin committed in the garden of Eden, but the potential to sin was possible through humans via their freedom to choose. Keeping true to God's method of operation, the serpent was made and identified as the shrewdest of all the animals, implying that he was cunning, clever with tricky awareness, did those attributes open the door for him to sin against God. What are your thoughts?

This is a narrative of the Israelites' drunken, rebellious lifestyle against the teaching of God's Word by Isaiah. They complained his method of teaching was repetitive: "He tells us everything over and over—one line at a time, one line at a time, a little here, and a little there!" (Isaiah 28:10). However, the method used by Isaiah was approved by God: "So the Lord will spell out his message for them again, one line at a time, one line at a time, a little here, and a little there" (Isaiah 28:13). We would be wise to search the scriptures as outlined in this verse. I think this is golden advice.

Let's take one line of scripture at a time from the Old and New Testaments, align one with another, and take the truths from each, a little here, and a little there, compile them into a structure of truth, and thus explain the catastrophe in the garden of Eden. I am not suggesting adding to or taking away from scriptures, God's Word; I see this as a process of supporting a truth repetitiously as stated in Isaiah's narrative. Are you ready to journey with me? Let's go!

How did the conversation between the woman and the serpent happen? Was conversing a normal routine for them? We can speculate that there had been no previous acts of evil perpetrated in the garden, so the woman would not have responded fearfully when the serpent began communicating with her. He started the conversation with a question: "Did God really say you must not eat the fruit from any of the trees in the garden?" The serpent's phrasing of the question was not what God had told the man and woman; it was a subtle way of provoking her to respond.

We know why God created the woman, but the serpent is a mystery other than he was an animal. Where did he get the authority to confront his overseer in this manner? We must investigate who the serpent really was and where he got his boldness. How many times had he seen the woman, and why did he choose that time to confront her with that question? What made the timing right?

The question he presented was a lie, but to sound legit, he mentioned God to prevent the woman from feeling uncomfortable and becoming defensive. He would have seen the man and the woman eating fruit from the other trees and known that God had not forbidden that.

The woman responded with the correct answer to show her knowledge and her desire to share it because of her felt need for self-recognition. It was a teaching moment for her.

> Of course we may eat the fruit from the trees in the garden. It's only the fruit from the tree in the middle of the garden that we are not allowed to eat. God said, "you must not eat it or even touch it; if you do, you will die."

She added something God had not said: "… or even touch it." She felt compelled to educate him with her knowledge, but I think she desired to enhance her answer as a value-added moment for her to feel good and portray her level of intelligence to the serpent.

What thoughts did that question generate in her heart? Remember that free will is driven by the natural and spiritual systems as they war against one another for control of the soul. He got her to become emotionally engrossed in the conversation because it was adding value to her. Her thoughts were shifting to the control of the natural system and arousing the fleshly desires that had led her to lie prior to eating the fruit.

He lied to her when he said in verse 4, "You won't die!" He was playing on her psychologically by personalizing her in his lie with the word *you*; he elevated himself above God by calling God a liar. In verse 5, the serpent realized he had completely moved the woman to her fleshly level of reasoning where there was no defense, only self-gratification.

He continued to attack God viciously unlike when he had mentioned God to get her to open the door; he said, "God knows that your eyes will be opened as soon as you eat it, and you will be like God, knowing both good and evil." True, God knew that their eyes would be opened and that they would become like the Godhead; that was why He warned them not to eat it.

The knowledge of good and evil was not the catchall for the woman; the trigger was pulled when the serpent told her she would be like God.

The serpent told a bald-faced lie mixed with truth. He sold a twisted lie to a woman controlled by her flesh; he made her believe she could be like God, and she acted on the lie. The serpent tempted, but she acted. What a travesty for humanity. What God took six days to create was destroyed in a 125-word conversation … Appalling!

Verse 6 reveals the results of the diabolical conversation. He was an experienced creature with the ability to beguile her. The serpent was shrewd but not a sinner. He would have shown his true character prior to this diabolical encounter with the woman. So what persuaded the serpent to become a sinner of lies? Let's look at the points.

1. The question was presented as a lie.
2. That is not the question an animal living in the garden would have asked.
3. She quantified her response by adding to the warning the word *touch*.
4. He told an outright lie: "You won't die!"
5. He elevated himself to a place above God by calling God a liar.
6. He continued to attack God viciously by making it appear humans could be like God by twisting the truth.

I conclude that the serpent was a manipulative liar controlled by the real perpetrator, one who hated God. The only supernatural being with the power to do that was Satan. Hold on! Don't abandon me; this is where we search the scriptural narratives "one line at a time, one line at a time, a little here, and a little there" for evidence that Satan was the true culprit who deceived the woman. He was wise enough to involve others in his devilish schemes. Evil loves company.

The scriptures highlight only one perpetrator who had the spiritual means, intelligence, and opportunity to plan and carry out his plan. There was hatred against God in his mind and heart. He had to have known God personally and started a feud with Him at some point. Ezekiel, a prophet of God, provided us with some very incriminating information about Satan in his symbolic, prophetic narrative of the king of Tyre as a type of Satan in Ezekiel 28:11–19.

Then this further message came to me from the Lord: "Son of man, sing this funeral song for the king of Tyre. Give him this message from the Sovereign Lord "You were the model of perfection, full of wisdom and exquisite in beauty. You were in Eden, the garden of God. Your clothing was adorned with every precious stone—red carnelian, pale-green peridot, white moonstone, blue-green beryl, onyx, green jasper, blue lapis lazuli, turquoise, and emerald—all beautifully crafted for you and set in the finest gold. They were given to you on the day you were created. I ordained and anointed you as the mighty angelic guardian. You had access to the holy mountain of God and walked among the stones of fire. "You were blameless in all you did from the day you were created until the day evil was found in you. Your rich commerce led you to violence, and you sinned. So I banished you in disgrace from the mountain of God. I expelled you, O mighty guardian, from your place among the stones of fire. Your heart was filled with pride because of all your beauty. Your wisdom was corrupted by your love of splendor. So I threw you to the ground and exposed you to the curious gaze of kings. You defiled your sanctuaries with your many sins and your dishonest trade. So I brought fire out from within you, and it consumed you. I reduced you to ashes on the ground in the sight of all who were watching. All who knew you are appalled at your fate. You have come to a terrible end, and you will exist no more."

This was a prophetic indictment of the king of Tyre. Satan had been created by God and had been in the garden of Eden. This mighty angel had access to the holy mountain of God with freedom of movement. Evil was in his heart; he had been banished in disgrace. His wisdom was corrupt and resulted in his being thrown to the ground by God. This behavior alone and the impending punishment would make him hate God. Based on this information, we can say with certainty that Satan was a fallen angel who had the power to control the serpent. He was also the first recorded sinner having been cast down for his sins but not yet destroyed. He has been God's evil nemesis throughout the ages. However, note that Ezekiel's prophecy from God has an eternal damnation appointment for Satan in the future.

Let's continue to compile line upon line here a little and there a little. In Isaiah 14:12–17, we read Satan's history.

> How you are fallen from heaven, O shining star, son of the morning! You have been thrown down to the earth, you who destroyed the nations of the world. For you said to yourself, "I will ascend to heaven and set my throne above God's stars. I will preside on the mountain of the gods far away in the north. I will climb to the highest heavens and be like the Most High." Instead, you will be brought down to the place of the dead, down to its lowest depths. Everyone there will stare at you and ask, "Can this be the one who shook the earth and made the kingdoms of the world tremble? Is this the one who destroyed the world and made it into a wasteland? Is this the king who demolished the world's greatest cities and had no mercy on his prisoners?"

This prophetic information help solidify our identity of Satan as the evil perpetrator who deceived the woman. Satan is evil and will try to destroy all of us because we were created in God's image and likeness and we are God's associates on earth. Revelation 12:3–4 and 7–9 corroborates this concept.

> Then I witnessed in heaven another significant event. I saw a large red dragon with seven heads and ten horns, with seven crowns on his heads. His tail swept away one-third of the stars in the sky, and he threw them to the earth. He stood in front of the woman as she was about to give birth, ready to devour her baby as soon as it was born.

> Then there was war in heaven. Michael and his angels
> fought against the dragon and his angels. And the dragon
> lost the battle, and he and his angels were forced out of
> heaven. This great dragon—the ancient serpent called the
> devil, or Satan, the one deceiving the whole world—was
> thrown down to the earth with all his angels.

Satan, the master manipulator, convinced a third of the angels to follow him in his attempt to overthrow God. The revealed truths provide us with the perpetrator's aliases that support our identifying him as the culprit: "dragon, ancient serpent (wonder why he chose the serpent), called the devil, or Satan." What a revelation! We can conclude he chose the serpent because he was identified by the same name. He was not a stranger to the earth since God had cast him down to it. We do not know when that happened, but we can surmise it was ages before God gave the earth a makeover. Regardless, Satan was present and not the serpent. Let's review one more scripture narrative before we give our closing position.

> For you are the children of your father the devil, and you
> love to do the evil things he does. He was a murderer from
> the beginning. He has always hated the truth, because
> there is no truth in him. When he lies, it is consistent
> with his character; for he is a liar and the father of lies. So
> when I tell the truth, you just naturally don't believe me!
> (John 8:44–45)

Here, Jesus identified Satan as a liar and the father of lies. Lying is Satan's method of operation to tempt anyone associated with God and in particular angels, humans, and animals. We must know his devices as warned in Isaiah 32:7 (ESV): "As for the scoundrel—his devices are evil; he plans wicked schemes to ruin the poor with lying words, even when the plea of the needy is right." 2 Corinthians 2:11 (NKJV), states, "… lest Satan should take advantage of us; for we are not ignorant of his devices."

Satan uses lies to tempt his victims to act against God's righteousness and decency. Satan will always attack the truth by twisting it with his lies to tempt his victims through their fleshly thoughts and emotions. Satan has perfected his knowledge of humankind for evil, and it is time we research and know about him so we can resist him and become more than conquerors of his lying schemes.

> Submit yourselves therefore to God. Resist the devil, and he will flee from you. (Walk in this verse and you will walk victorious over Satan, by crushing his head!). (James 4:7 KJV)

> For if God did not spare the angels who sinned, but cast *them* down to hell and delivered *them* into chains of darkness, to be reserved for judgment; and did not spare the ancient world, but saved Noah, *one of* eight *people,* a preacher of righteousness, bringing in the flood on the world of the ungodly; and turning the cities of Sodom and Gomorrah into ashes, condemned *them* to destruction, making *them* an example to those who afterward would live ungodly; and delivered righteous Lot, *who was* oppressed by the filthy conduct of the wicked (for that righteous man, dwelling among them, tormented *his* righteous soul from day to day by seeing and hearing *their* lawless deeds) *then* the Lord knows how to deliver the godly out of temptations and to reserve the unjust under punishment for the day of judgment. (2 Peter 2:4–9 NKJV)

For a stay focused review, Satan's characteristics identified in scripture align with the characteristics identified in the conversation assessment: the perpetrator was a liar with the power, wisdom, and supernatural means to enter the garden and possess the serpent. He had the experience to execute the plan. He had ages of sinful hatred and ongoing warfare against God. I am convinced that we have more than enough factual evidence to establish Satan as the evil perpetrator who deceived the woman.

The deception of the woman had eternal consequences unlike the world would ever face again—the unleashing of evil on every created structure of God. Genesis 3:6 reads,

The woman was convinced. She saw that the tree was beautiful, and its fruit looked delicious, and she wanted the wisdom it would give her. So she took the fruit and ate it. Then she gave some to her husband, who was with her, and he ate it, too.

Satan convinced the woman that his lies were the truth. Believing and entertaining sin makes one sinful. Proverbs 23:7 (KJV) states it this way: "For as he thinketh in his heart ..." Her natural system was controlling her, and she entered the sinful realm. Once the natural system is in control, one becomes blind to the truth. Romans 8:5–8 (KJV) explains what happened to the woman.

Stop

Those who are dominated by the sinful nature think about sinful things, but those who are controlled by the Holy Spirit think about things that please the Spirit. So letting your sinful nature control your mind leads to death. But letting the Spirit control your mind leads to life and peace. For the sinful nature is always hostile to God. It never did obey God's laws, and it never will. That's why those who are still under the control of their sinful nature can never please God.

Satan's sinful lies seduced the woman into sin. In her sinful nature, she saw the tree different from God's description and warning. Sin distorts humans' ability to rationalize in an orderly and decent manner. Sin makes everything appear better than it is. The beautiful tree became even more beautiful. The fruit looked better to her than ever. The thought of being "wise as God" made the fruit more desirable. Satan stirred her need for self-actualization and left her only one appropriate action—eat the fruit. We can infer the woman used the same sinful lies Satan used to convince her on her man causing him to eat the fruit without challenging her. The sin of lying is contagious and loves company.

Since we have disclosed Satan's method of operation, we have no reason to be ignorant of his devices as stated by the apostle Paul in 2 Corinthians 2:11. He took advantage of the woman and man resulting in a monumental and devastating loss through death; we must not become victims of his method of operation. Satan is not omnipresent (all present), omnipotent (all powerful), or omniscient (all knowing), so he had to devise a strategy to deceive other created beings into following him, he did that by lying, and lies can mobilize an army of deceived followers and supporters that can make Satan appear to be omnipresent, omnipotent, and omniscient.

The sinful nature of man hungers for the leadership of its father, Satan, who disguises God's truths and infiltrates lives to follow him after seducing them with his subtle lies. He is forever innovating his lying schemes through the art of deception. He is currently using a technique called conspiracy theories, speculations derived from abstract reasoning to accomplish an illegal or ill-fated outcome. They are used to entice others to join other participants in bringing the theory to fruition. Conspiracy theories are nothing more than decorated lies that appear to be based on a legal principle; that is why he misuses scriptures out of context. His lies confuse and create chaotic outcomes of evil in the lives of humankind. They are devised to destroy, steal, and kill those who are targeted out of hatred, fear, jealousy, greed, malicious competition, and simply deception.

Children of God must guard themselves against satanic evil. The apostle Paul stated in his letter to the Galatians 3:1 (KJV), "O foolish Galatians, who hath bewitched you, that ye should not obey the truth, before whose eyes Jesus Christ hath been evidently set forth, crucified among you?" This statement identifies the devastating impact conspiracy theories can have on individuals.

Let's explore the word *bewitched*. According to *The New Testament Practical Word Study*, the word *bewitched* means to fascinate, cast a spell upon, mislead, deceive[3] The word *foolish* implies being controlled or acting upon misinformation made to appear reasonable and truthful. Conspiracy theories always have ulterior motives to benefit the makers of such decorated lies. The motive is to divert the hearts of children of God from godly to human values disguised as God's truths; it focuses attention on an individual, an organization, a philosophical viewpoint, or a unique

---

[3] *Leadership Ministries Worldwide. (1996). Galatians–Colossians (p. 37). Chattanooga, TN: Leadership Ministries Worldwide.*
1*The American Heritage Dictionary of the English Language. 4th Edition Boston: Houghton Mifflin. 2000, S.V. "humanism."*

The Catastrophe in the Garden

people through humanism; According to *The American Heritage College Dictionary*, humanism means "A system of thought centering on humans and their values, capacities, and worth and deemphasizing religious beliefs." That is the deceptive motive of Satan operating through duped or charmed humans under his powers that cause chaos and confusion. Neither humans nor their accomplishments can offer eternal life because they are all temporary.

Not so with the God of our salvation through Jesus Christ. He is the same yesterday, today, and forever. He is all the security we need, so we should never let anyone dupe us into following another human and not even ourselves—only Jesus through the truth of His Word.

After Satan tempted the woman, he left the scene because he accomplished his mission—seducing her into believing his lies, which caused her to doubt the command of God. I dwell on this point to prevent us from following the path of our first parents, a path Satan will attempt to victimize us on so that our lives will not glorify God but lead to our death. We must learn from our first parents and not be ignorant of Satan's devices because he hates us as God's precious trophies.

When Satan attacks you, submit yourself to God and acknowledge His lordship with praise and spiritual songs, quote scriptures that exalt Him and your loving passion for Him, and always pray in the Spirit. These divine actions will cause Satan to flee you and will draw you closer to God. Resistance is most effective when we express our love for our Heavenly Father while rejoicing over how great He is.

Satan cannot compete with a child of God who exalts Him in the midst of his attacks because he is not receiving any attention or acknowledgment while executing his sinful devices. We resist Satan by giving our undivided attention to the awesome God of our salvation. We do not give Satan a passageway to our hearts because he has already been defeated and judged by God. He is a loser and we are winners through Jesus Christ.

Live in the Spirit of faith in Jesus, and fear not when you are tempted and experience suffering because God will not give you more than you are able to handle. Always stand on God's truths, a solid foundation for victory over your enemies.

The events continue in Genesis 3:7: "At that moment their eyes were opened, and they suddenly felt shame at their nakedness. So they sewed fig leaves together to cover themselves." "Their eyes were opened" refers not to their physical eyes but to their evil spiritual eyes. In Matthew 6:22–23, Jesus stated,

> Your eye is a lamp that provides light for your body. When your eye is good, your whole body is filled with light. But when your eye is bad, your whole body is filled with darkness. And if the light you think you have is actually darkness, how deep that darkness is!

Jesus was referring to eyes as a type of heart, mind, and soul, the spiritual system of righteousness and holiness. The eye is the filter for light to enter the heart to the degree it is open. A closed eye lets in no light, and a fully opened eye lets it all in.

"Their eyes were opened" meant that their days of innocence had come to an end and that evil then shared the seat of knowledge with humankind. Humans previously had the veil of righteousness and holiness alone; however, when they ate the forbidden fruit, they inherited the veil of evil. Humankind now possesses the knowledge of good and evil with only one eye to focus through at a time. When the eye is good, our souls or lives are filled with light (always victorious); when the eye is evil, our souls or lives are filled with darkness (always defeat).

John 8:12 states, "Jesus spoke to the people once more and said, 'I am the light of the world. If you follow me, you won't have to walk in darkness, because you will have the light that leads to life.'" Jesus has since become the eye of good (light) to replace the contaminated eye of evil (darkness).

Genesis 3:7 reveals that the consequences of their sin, eating the fruit, were immediate; their eyes were opened. They had operated in the system of order and decency, righteousness, and holiness, and had been in harmony with God. They had lived free of laws and sin. Evil was not present in the garden, so they had had no need to be ashamed or embarrassed.

The tree of the knowledge of good and evil had a godly purpose. The word *good* defines God's righteousness and holiness and His love for humanity. It promotes life. The word *evil* denotes wickedness, the opposite of good; evil is the very nature of Satan. It promotes death. The tree was unique in that it offered two opposing systems simultaneously—the knowledge of good and evil. The tree paralleled the creative system of God; man was created with two systems, the natural (visible) and the spiritual (invisible) that work together. Good was the only nature present during man's time in the garden prior to eating the forbidden fruit because there was no knowledge of evil. When man and woman ate the fruit, their eyes were opened to evil. The knowledge of good unfortunately then coexisted with the knowledge of evil. Galatians 5:17 explains this precisely.

> The sinful nature wants to do evil, which is just the opposite of what the Spirit wants. And the Spirit gives us desires that are the opposite of what the sinful nature desires. These two forces are constantly fighting each other, so you are not free to carry out your good intentions.

The only way Adam and Eve could have prevented evil from making its appearance was to obey God by not eating the forbidden fruit. The knowledge of good and evil derailed their relationship with God and humankind. The two natures are enemies fighting for control of the soul because they cannot control it at the same time. God will not dwell in an unclean temple; exactly what humankind had become.

The sinful nature immediately took control, and they felt shame at their nakedness. Their bodies, which God had fearfully and wonderfully made in His image, were a source of shame for them, so they covered themselves with leaves. This is the appropriate time for us to revisit Genesis 2:25: "And they were both naked, the man and his wife, and were not ashamed"; back then, they were in the spirit realm and at harmony with God, but when they entered the natural realm, they felt shame. Romans 8:5 explains this crucial life truth: "Those who are dominated by the sinful nature think about sinful things, but those who are controlled by the Holy Spirit think about things that please the Spirit."

God had given Adam and Eve free will, the essence of humankind that presents it the greatest challenge to living sin-free lives. Our compassionate God provided a way to victory despite our sinful nature so we could honor and be in fellowship with Him. Since sinful flesh cannot glory in the sight of God, it had to be banished from God's presence. In 1 Corinthians 1:29 (KJV), states, "No flesh should glory in his presence."

Humanism became the order of life for dysfunctional human structures that excluded God, who is truth as stated in Deuteronomy 32:4 (KJV): "*He is* the Rock, his work *is* perfect: for all his ways *are* judgment: a God of truth and without iniquity, just and right *is* he."

Lying is Satan's primary weapon in his battle with truth. There can be no confusion if there is no truth; without truth, there would be no target to attack. To birth an opportunity to confuse you requires a truth—order and decency. A state of order and decency is established by a governing person, board, or government. What that person or body adopts as truth becomes truth to the followers, and God created the earth and its inhabitants based on truth for His honor and glory. The Godhead is the governing body that established truth to control the order and moral conduct of humankind.

God communicated only one truth to man and woman—that they should not eat the fruit of the tree of the knowledge of good and evil, but Satan convinced the woman and the woman convinced the man to disobey that one truth, and they descended into a state of confusion and dysfunction\ resulting in their death. Normalcy is based on compliance to the truth, and abnormality is based on noncompliance to the truth. The lie provided her with options she had never explored before that caused her to forget her purpose. Lies can become very convincing when confusion sets in. They humanize by drawing attention to self while presenting false pictures of victory, self- accomplishments, riches, prominent status, grandiose recognitions, and so on; they blind the truth with fake, selfish, and elaborate returns, advantages, and outcomes. Unfortunately, they work because the sinful mind embraces them resulting in the flesh responding to the evil deceptions through acts of sin.

We must guard our minds and resist temptation with the truth, the Word of God, which will always free us from evil. Jesus stated in John 8:32, "And you will know the truth, and the truth will set you free." The truth is our way to the heart of God and is our best weapon against Satan. I challenge you to know God and His ways through your practical knowledge of His truths.

There is only one governing power humankind should live by—God through His truths. Satan does not have any truths; he only attacks God's truths. His one and only objective is to prevent humanity from following God's truths because he hates God and His associates.

It is important to test the truth to discover its context. There is only one source of truth, God, and He always places His truth in context to maintain its order. The test is simple; compare what you are told to the truths of God, search the scriptures in context, and rely on confirmation from the Holy Spirit. If what you are told is not in context with God's truths, do not honor it, because truth out of context is deception.

1 John 4:1, states, "Dear friends, do not believe everyone who claims to speak by the Spirit. You must test them to see if the spirit they have comes from God. For there are many false prophets in the world." Satan knows the scriptures and will attempt to deceive you by taking the scriptures out of context and completely changing their purpose. He will try to dupe you into focusing on self or other humans through false pretenses rather than on God through Jesus Christ. Search the scriptures and seek direction from God through His Spirit before you commit to anything. God's peace in your spirit is an indicator that you are doing what honors Him. If you experience doubt or uncertainty, do not act; back off, wait on the Lord for directions, and seek advice from someone you honor and trust to confirm what is in your heart. Make sure your decisions align with God's truth in context.

The apostle Paul taught us how to prepare for warfare with Satan in Ephesians 6:17: "Put on salvation as your helmet, and take the sword of the Spirit, which is the word of God." His Word is our offensive weapon in spiritual warfare. We must apply the Word to our daily lives so we can spot Satan's lies. He wants us to misapply God's Word and thus become dysfunctional and fall under his control. Remember Jesus made Satan flee by quoting scripture back to him in context.

Children of God must know Him and His ways through the scriptures and follow Jesus's teachings and example. They must feed their spirits on the Word of God so they can master it and have it readily available in their times of need. The Word brings them freedom from fear, sin, and death through building up their faith in and passion for God, Jesus, and the Holy Spirit. They must see the value of God's truths and allow them to resonate in their hearts. Freedom can be experienced only through God's truths; we study them to show ourselves faithful to the Godhead.

Let's continue with the catastrophe in the garden.

> When the cool evening breezes were blowing, the man and his wife heard the LORD God walking about in the garden. So they hid from the LORD God among the trees. Then the LORD God called to the man, "Where are you?" He replied, "I heard you walking in the garden, so I hid. I was afraid because I was naked." "Who told you that you were naked?" the LORD God asked. "Have you eaten from the tree whose fruit I commanded you not to eat?" The man replied, "It was the woman you gave me who gave me the fruit, and I ate it." Then the LORD God asked the woman, "What have you done?" "The serpent deceived me," she replied. "That's why I ate it." (Genesis 3:8–13)

Note how the sinful nature functioned at the onset of humankind's rebellion against God; things have changed little. When the man and woman heard God walking in the garden, they hid from Him; they had disobeyed Him and did not want to face the consequences, and that response became normal for human beings. The sinful mind devises many ungodly acts and then attempts to hide after they are carried out because it knows those acts are sinful. The sinful nature is not deterred by the threat of punishment; it is diabolically driven to engage in evil behavior, its nature. Our first parents committed sin and then tried to hide, which was another sin.

When God asked, "Where are you?" the man came out because he realized he could not hide from God. His response was out of the ordinary. He hid because he was naked, which made him afraid, but that was no reason to fear God, who had created him naked. Adam's was a sinful, fleshly response to keep him from confessing his disobedience. Fear is another tool Satan uses; it is the spirit of the sinful nature that results in uncontrolled behavior and panicked responses such as worrying, troubled mindsets, and stress in anticipation of danger. Satan instills fear in people to destroy them without ever touching them. Fear is not from God; 2 Timothy 2:7 (KJV) states, "For God hath not given us the spirit of fear; but of power, and of love, and of a sound mind." God imparts power, love, and soundness of mind to His children so the fear of evil will not victimize them.

In Genesis 3:11, God asked Adam and Eve, "Who told you that you were naked? Have you eaten from the tree whose fruit I commanded you not to eat?" God was displaying His grace to the man and woman; He knew what they had done; He knows all things even before they happen. He had tested the man and woman by giving Satan access to them. He knew that they would not pass the test and that He would address the matter with them for the benefit of those in the coming ages. He later allowed Satan to test Job and Jesus; see Job 1:6–12 and Matthew 4:1–11 in the scripture index at the end of this book, perfect examples of God allowing Satan to test his servants.

God tested me through my flesh, the world, and Satan a number of times. I passed some, and I failed some only to be retested. God's testing is not done for His own knowledge because He knows the heart of all human beings before they act; it is a test for people to know where they stand in relationship with God per His truths. This is a demonstration of God's love for His creation, His way of keeping us abreast of our life journey with Him. If we misstep, His grace gives us the chance to be restored by repenting and confessing our sins as stated in 1 John 1:9 (KJV): "If we confess our sins, he is faithful and just to forgive us our sins, and to cleanse us from all unrighteousness." This truth is a grace blessing from God to His children. I encourage you to harness it in your heart because opportunities for you to use it will come. We have a faithful and forgiving Heavenly Father who loves us. Please do not sin against God willfully thinking you have 1 John 1:9 to fall back on; the wages of sin are still death when you know you should do good but choose to do evil.

The man and woman did not answer God's question about their nakedness; their only response would have been that no one had told them that, that they had seen their nakedness themselves. And the answer to the second question would have to be, "Yes, we ate it." Both answers would have been admissions of guilt. They did not respond with broken and contrite hearts; rather, he blamed her and she blamed the serpent. The sinful nature always looks for a way out even in the face of truth because the penalty for sin is death.

Can you imagine what the world would be like if our first parents had confessed their sins rather than bringing more damnation on themselves and for all to follow?

Stop When Adam said, "It was the woman you gave me who gave me the fruit, and I ate it," he was trying to shift the blame onto her and God alike. What a conniving response. He had free will and could have rejected the fruit. His sin was not being tempted but giving in to the temptation and thus being disobedient to God.

God moved on to the woman, who blamed the serpent for deceiving her and said, "That's why I ate it." The lying continued. The serpent did not tell her to eat the fruit, he lied about what would not happen if she ate it. It was her free will to choose good or evil, and her sinful mind convinced her to eat the fruit so she would receive its alleged benefits. Every human being can choose to obey God and receive eternal life or disobey Him and receive eternal damnation.

Sin caused Adam and Eve to rebel against God despite the fact He had provided them with everything they needed. However, God had not destroyed His nemesis, Satan; He allowed Satan, His adversary, to roam the cosmos. To battle Satan and his minions, we must learn all we can about him. Let's explore the way he operates. One thing is sure—Satan does not want to be known as the enemy of God and humankind. He loves to operate incognito so he can continue to deceive people into thinking he does not exist, that he is only a cute fairytale that trots around in a red jumpsuit with a pitchfork in hand. Unfortunately, he is celebrated and worshiped by many cults. 1 John 3:8–9 (NKJV) states, He who sins is of the devil, for the devil has sinned from the beginning. For this purpose the Son of God was manifested, that He might destroy the works of the devil. Those who have been born into God's family do not make a practice of sinning, because God's life is in them. So they can't keep on sinning, because they are children of God.

But Satan has been exposed. We can resist him and walk in the truth Jesus provides us; He is the key to eternal life. The devil does not want that truth to be told. Let's expose him for what he is. There are approximately twenty-one names he is known by in the holy Bible, the most noted being Satan (adversary), devil (slanderer), Lucifer (light bearer, shining one, the son of the morning), and old serpent.

His main tool, lying, results in deception, craftiness, trickery, cunningness, cleverness, shrewdness, hatred, and so on. He wants to destroy God and anyone associated with Him. Satan is blatantly evil and wicked and must be hated by children of God. That hatred should be displayed through exalting God and sharing His love and Son, Jesus, with everyone. If we truly hate evil, we will act to destroy it by sharing with others how to escape and overcome it with good. Love always triumphs over evil.

Satan was expelled from the kingdom of God because he attempted to overthrow God, His creator. He has freedom to roam the earth seeking victims to devour. He has several titles of authority, such as the ruler of this world; John 12:31 states, "The time for judging this world has come, when Satan, the ruler of this world, will be cast out."

Let's look to the *Practical Word Study of The New Testament* as a source to help us grasp further insight and knowledge of our arch enemy Satan.

> Let's look at the terminology Jesus used when he called Satan "the prince of this world" (John 16:11 KJV). 1The word *prince* in ancient Greek was *archon*, a ruler." The word "world" is the Greek word *Kosmos*, which emphatically does *not* describe the earth, universe, or planetary systems. Instead, it denotes *culture, society,* and the *systems* in which mankind lives and functions. It denotes systems, such as education, entertainment, government, and every human sphere, as the places—the *Kosmos*—where Satan operates. The word *Kosmos* is the identical word that the apostle Paul used in 2 Corinthians 4:4 (KJV) when he referred to Satan as the "god of this world." It pictures Satan as being the ruler of the lost culture and lost systems that dominates every sphere of mankind. Those systems are where Satan temporarily operates and exercises his power.

1 Peter 5:8, states, "Stay alert! Watch out for your great enemy, the devil. He prowls around like a roaring lion, looking for someone to devour." Ephesians 6:12 says, "We are not fighting against flesh-and-blood enemies, but against evil rulers and authorities of the unseen world, against mighty powers in this dark world, and against evil spirits in the heavenly places."

1 Leadership Ministries Worldwide. 2004. The Practical Word Studies of the New Testament. Page: 2293, L- #376; prince, world.

Satan has been judged by Jesus and has a date with the Lake of Fire, but until that time, he will be a deadly enemy of God and everything and everyone associated with Him. Jesus identified

Satan's mission and purpose in John 10:10: "The thief's purpose is to steal and kill and destroy." Inflicting evil on God's creation is the sole intent of Satan and his minions. This warfare will continue until God casts him into hell and finally into the Lake of Fire for eternity.

Satan inflicted a devastating wound on humankind when he deceived our first parents. They were created perfect and good, but they were not sealed from sin or Satan. Satan deceived them and planted the seed of evil within them. Unfortunately, it took root in their hearts; as a result, sin was imputed upon all humanity. Romans 5:12 states, "When Adam sinned, sin entered the world. Adam's sin brought death, so death spread to everyone, for everyone sinned."

What has impacted you most about the catastrophe in the garden of Eden? Have you learned anything from our first parents that has helped shape your life? How has Satan attempted to destroy your life?

CHAPTER 15

The Cost of Sin

Sin always has consequences, and they always exceed the temporary pleasures of sinful acts. Genesis 3:14 speaks to this: Then the LORD God said to the serpent, 'Because you have done this, you are cursed more than all animals, domestic and wild. You will crawl on your belly, groveling in the dust as long as you live.'"

God issued punishment to the violators. The first was the serpent. The narrative does not name the sinful act committed by the serpent; God stated simply, "Because you have done this"; perhaps the sin was that the serpent had allowed Satan to possess him. We have scriptures that say Satan and his demons could possess animals as well as humans. (Please refer to the scripture index for this chapter.)

The serpent was not Satan; he was an available vessel Satan used to deceive the woman. The punishment he received was due to his having been a voluntary participant in Satan's scheme. God cursed him more than all animals and made him crawl on his belly. That leaves us with the impression that the serpent had been created to walk upright since his punishment demoted him to crawling.

Misery loves company. Satan's strategy to undermine God included others who would do his dirty work of persuading others to sin. It was easy for me when I was growing up to become involved in evil acts with my friends. One would suggest committing a mischievous act, and one by one, we would all agree. One time after a Thursday night Boy Scout meeting, we were influenced to go to the railroad tracks and throw stones at tractor-trailers traveling on the highway. We intentionally targeted the trailers and not the tractor, but once the rocks left our hands, we had no control over them. Throwing rocks became routine for us after our Scout meetings; think about it—Boy Scouts committing acts of destruction. It shows how easily evil crept in and undermined all the good we had been taught.

One night when we were poised to assault the trucks, a dozen vehicles turned their bright lights on us. Several of the guys were caught and taken to their parents, but I escaped. The next day at school, we were all called to the principal's office by name over the intercom and confronted by the police chief and Mr. Mickens, our principal, whom I respected. We were sternly warned about our reckless actions and the consequences if we committed the evil act again. We were told of the imminent danger we posed to the drivers. How easy it had been for us to persuade one another to engage in a dangerous act immediately after repeating the Boy Scout's Code of Honor. But even as a young adult, I was persuaded and persuaded others to engage in evil acts. Sin very seldom acts alone.

Satan does not work alone; he is always recruiting others and even some in the church to engage in his evil work with him. Unfortunately, we blame one another for the evil acts we commit when Satan, the mastermind behind it all, is not even considered. Many times, God is blamed for allowing the sin to occur, a repeat of our first parents' behavior. We children of God must know the devices of Satan and not give him a free pass by blaming others for our sins. We must assist one another when we fall into temptation and trials on this journey to eternal life. If we work together as each other's keepers, we will cause Satan to flee so that no one will perish because of his deceptions.

Seek wise and godly counsel when going through difficult seasons in your life so you can be strengthened. Please do not attempt to fight the battle alone. Satan uses this technique to bring us down by recruiting others to his side, and it unfortunately works for him. We should use God's truth and reach out to others so we can reinforce our efforts to resist the world, the flesh, and Satan. Two working together are better than one; the greater the number of strands in a cord, the stronger it becomes. Let's unite for the sake of our love for God and one another.

What are your thoughts concerning the punishment of the serpent? What are your thoughts about Satan's use of the serpent? Have you made yourself available to help those who are facing challenges?

CHAPTER 16

The Hostility between the Two Seeds

Genesis 3:15, states, "And I will cause hostility between you and the woman, and between your offspring and her offspring. He will strike your head, and you will strike his heel," is considered the promise verse of salvation by many Bible scholars because of the catastrophe in the garden, and I agree with that. God shifted His attention to the ancient serpent, Satan, per Revelation 20:2. I consider this verse to be God's prophetic end to the reign of Satan.

God's plan of salvation included the end of Satan, His nemesis. Destroying Satan is the only way sin could be removed from the cosmos. God's plan of salvation was first revealed in Genesis 3:15 and continued to the book of Revelation. Satan has been judged, and his time of reckoning is drawing closer.

Let's explore the good news this verse brings. God informed Satan that the battle was on between them through the seed of the woman. What is the implication? In the first round of the battle, it appeared that Satan had won and that the woman had lost. However, God said in essence, "Hold on! We're just getting started with my plan to rid my cosmos of you and your minions." God put Satan on notice by laying out the path to his demise. God's punishment included causing enmity between the two;

the woman and Satan would hate and oppose each other. Satan's weapon against her was sin and death, and her weapon against him was God's truths; it was a battle between good and evil.

The battles were waged both in the natural, visible system and the spiritual, invisible system. The entire world is impacted by this spiritual warfare of hostility because its focus was on human beings, whom Satan has deceived into thinking that their enemy was their fellow man. Such a depraved mentality results from the catastrophe in the garden. Open our eyes, dear God, that we might fight the real enemy, Satan, with the actual weapons of our secured salvation, your truths.

God continued to hand out His judgment upon the two by including their offspring in this hostile relationship. He explained the roles they would play. Satan's offspring (sin and death) would strike the heel of the woman's offspring, and the woman's offspring (Jesus) would strike and crush the head of Satan's offspring. These two crucial blows will solidify the division between the two.

Notice the locations of the blows—the heel and the head. It is obvious which blow would be more devastating. God has fulfilled this truth through Jesus, the offspring born of a virgin and who was crucified—the blow to His heel. However, the woman's offspring rose from the dead victorious over sin and death, the blow to the head that defeated Satan and his offspring. Satan has been judged, declared guilty, and sentenced to eternity in the Lake of Fire, amen!

> Because God's children are human beings—made of flesh and blood—the Son also became flesh and blood. For only as a human being could he die, and only by dying could he break the power of the devil, who had the power of death. Only in this way could he set free all who have lived their lives as slaves to the fear of dying. (Hebrews 2:14–15)

> O death, where is your victory? O death, where is your sting?" For sin is the sting that results in death, and the law gives sin its power. But thank God! He gives us victory over sin and death through our Lord Jesus Christ. (1 Corinthians 15:55–57)

These verses define the present and future of the believer's victory resulting from the warfare between the seed of the woman and the seed of Satan. Jesus has given us the victory over sin and death because of His resurrection from the dead after the blow to His heel, His death on the cross where His blood was shed as payment for the sins of all who would believe in Him. "He is risen!" is the shout of victory over death.

Hostilities between the followers of good and the followers of evil have affected all humanity throughout the ages. Satan has caused different ethnic groups to hate one another because they are not like them, and this has resulted in the inhumane deaths inflicted upon one another by senseless wars. He has birthed hatred among family members even to the point of murder. Jesus stated that Satan's mission was to "kill, steal, and destroy" everything associated with God, including humanity. He can infiltrate families, friendships, workplaces, governments, nations, and organizations of all types, including the church, and thus cause confusion, hatred, and evil. Wherever people are, Satan is, and he is spreading his poison.

The only way to eternal victory is through Jesus Christ, not with hatred that causes divisions in families accompanied by sinful acts. This hostility will not cease until Satan's judgment is carried out by God when Satan is banished to the Lake of Fire his eternal home. Until then, we must continue steadfastly holding onto our desire for eternal life with God. As children of God we are called to live righteous and holy lives, which will position us for warfare against Satan and his followers, and to rescue those who are perishing under his power by sharing the good news of Jesus Christ, who has redeemed us through His death and resurrection from the dead. Therefore, providing eternal life to those who believe in Him!

We cannot stop all hatred and evil, but we can make a difference for those God places in our paths on our journeys to eternal life. Warfare results in many being killed and wounded physically and mentally; spiritual warfare is different in the sense that the battle never ceases until God calls us home. Therefore, children of God must prepare themselves to endure for a lifetime of warfare against evil adversaries.

The most essential part of preparing for spiritual warfare is to realize we can do nothing without Jesus, so we must trust in and focus on Him alone. He is our only true and trusted friend who will carry us to victory.

We must get to know Him and His ways and then surrender our lives into His hands. Only Jesus can deliver us from our afflictions into the hands of God. He will always be there for us even when we cannot feel or see Him. When we face trials, tribulations and sufferings we must keep our eyes fixed on Jesus who will deliver us out of them all. Remember we are only strangers passing through this life as witnesses of Jesus on our way to our heavenly home. We are not afraid of death because we have eternal life through Jesus Christ and death only transport us home to forever be with our Heavenly Father and family.

With that knowledge your power is released when you rely solely on the truths of God. You must live daily as a warring soldier who trusts God's Word as your compass. The Word will never desert you; it is your strength, your sword, so use it in every battle. No battle is without suffering, anguish, and pain, but your outcome will always be victory. The life of a soldier in God's army is always sacrificial to the cause of Jesus—that none perish! Sacrificing always results in suffering to some degree, but the result will be honored with rewards from God Himself.

Allow your life to replicate Jesus's nature so that others will witness your rejoicing of thanksgiving for the victory of eternal life you have in Jesus. Life is not fair because of the hostility between good and the evil that victimizes us, but life is worth living because of God's goodness, which has rescued us from Satan. Righteousness, joy, and peace will be the order of the day for eternity for those who invite God to be their Heavenly Father through Jesus.

Keep falling in love with Jesus every day because He has secured eternal life for you. Embrace the eternal promised future God has for all who believe in Jesus and look forward to His return for you and others with overflowing expectations.

We must redirect our attention to the punishment God placed on the woman in Genesis 3:16: "I will sharpen the pain of your pregnancy, and in pain you will give birth. And you will desire to control your husband, but he will rule over you." Prior to then, the woman had not given birth under God's reproduction system: "Be fruitful and multiply" (Genesis 1:28). The unfortunate choice of the woman did not cancel her reproduction function; however, her behavior resulted in being punished with pain during pregnancy and giving birth, a punishment that would be passed down throughout the ages. Birthing today is a major medical concern because of the many challenges women face before and during delivery due to Eve's rebellion against God.

The second half of the punishment identifies another major challenge for the woman that would affect the man as well. Genesis 3:16 states, "The woman's desire will be to control her husband, but the husband will rule over her." Opposing forces will always be in conflict. The challenge is upon the wife and husband to walk in accordance with the truths of God so there would be peace in their marriage. Peace and happiness should be the desired outcome in every marriage. True peace and happiness must flow through God's truths for husband and wife.

Phyllis and I married at age twenty-one and have been married for fifty-one years. Unfortunately, I grew up without my father in the home; which put me at a grave disadvantage with no practical observations on how to build a peaceful and happy marriage. The first seven years of our marriage were tough because of my past challenging military life and service as a police officer. I was confused, and my allegiance was still to my friends. I could not adjust to married life because I did not know how. I was mentally still in Vietnam and enamored with being a police officer especially as a narcotics detective. I was not totally focused on my wife and our first child, Carnetha. I loved them, but my mind and lifestyle did not show that. I felt that as long as I provided housing, food, and transportation, I was fulfilling my marriage obligations.

My friends were not much help because we were all learning from one another how to make our marriages fail. I became consumed with living as a nonpracticing Christian and enjoying the pleasures of this evil world. Consuming alcohol followed me from Vietnam and was reinforced by my work as a police officer. Having a good time for me was hanging out with friends and going home drunk. I did not return to my Christian roots during the first seven years of my marriage.

Phyllis was a great wife; she tolerated me and my foolishness and stayed committed to her marriage vows even after I abruptly quit my job as a police officer after three and a half years without secured employment. I just flipped into confusion and needed to get away from myself and my out-of-control lifestyle.

After job jumping for a while, I enrolled in St. Petersburg Junior

College using my GI Bill to pay for my education. Surprisingly, I graduated with an associate arts degree after having dropped out twelve months earlier. I was basically attending to collect my veteran's benefits. God works in amazing ways when your family is praying for you.

I was motivated to attend Florida State University while my wife and daughter stayed with her mother. I met new friends and continued the partying life without my wife. Somehow, I completed my studies in eighteen months and earned a bachelor of science degree in criminology and criminal justice.

I joined my wife and daughter, who were living with her mother, Mom Sallie, and her sister, Josephine. I reconnected with my previous friends and continued living my confused life. I was unable to find full-time employment for five months. Phyllis had worked for a manufacturing company while I was attending school, and she continued that after I graduated. She was the breadwinner then. I could secure only a part-time job as a delivery driver. My friends chided me for having a college degree but no job. I never had to worry about alcohol and cigarettes because they kept me supplied with that.

But God was working through Phyllis. She was introduced to Jesus Christ by a coworker, the wife of a pastor. Phyllis invited Jesus into her life and became a student of God's Word relating to the end times. She would often share what she learned with me and challenge me to attend church with her. I told her I was not about to attend anyone's church in my condition, but she faithfully attended church with our daughter.

Many times, I felt like giving up. Nothing appeared to be working for me. I felt like a complete failure. I began to relive my failed life over and over, which always ended with drinking or smoking marijuana with friends to escape myself. I felt cheated and guilty for getting wounded in Vietnam too early in combat. My friend had died saving me … How could I ever repay that? I had simply walked off my job as a police officer for no reason. I could not get back into the military, and on top of that, I could not secure a decent job to support my wife and daughter Carnetha. My life was crashing quickly.

I thank God for my wife, who continued to believe and trust God for us both. Her life change and her knowledge of the Bible impressed me. She lit up when sharing the Word of God with me, but I was not there yet.

I finally secured a job in Fort Lauderdale, which required our relocating. We did not own any furniture or valuables; we had only our clothes and a car, but off we went. I enjoyed my job as an insurance adjustor and could afford a two-bedroom apartment. At that time, Phyllis and I had been married six years and were blessed with our second daughter, Eboni. We later added Kellie, Crystal, Ashley, and Zol-Licia.

In 1976, I had reached rock bottom. I was tired of me and could find no satisfaction or purpose in life even after securing decent employment. I would have pity parties and entertain ungodly thoughts. I had hurts that alcohol and smoking cigarettes and marijuana could not satisfy; my mind was always processing failure.

In spite of all the challenges, we were able to purchase a three-bedroom home. Phyllis had a job as a phlebotomist at a hospital, and one would think everything was falling into place. However, I felt lost and incomplete, and possessing things was not easing my pain. I continued trying to find resolve in alcohol.

A breakthrough began when Phyllis and the girls began attending a nondenominational Pentecostal church. She confronted me frequently by repeating a comment I had made to her a year earlier: "When you find a good church, I'll attend it." She told me that she had found such a church and invited me to attend with her and the girls. My response was brief and short: "OK, I will … soon."

She became a participant in a Bible study and invited me to attend, and I did. I enjoyed the study but felt uncomfortable. After a couple of visits, I felt the tugging to stop drinking liquor, and I did cold turkey after ten years; that was miracle number one. I had stopped smoking cigarettes cold turkey about six months earlier. However, I continued to consume beer. One day after purchasing a can of beer, I bumped into our pastor and felt embarrassed with the beer in hand. I had not made any commitments to him or Phyllis, but shame engulfed me, and I stopped attending. I know now it was the convicting power of the Holy Spirit.

The next Sunday, I attended a church service for the first time in years with Phyllis and my daughters. It felt great, and I enjoyed the service. I was excited about attending church the next Sunday to hear the pastor speak; that was miracle number two. My mother was visiting us that weekend and was excited about attending church with us, something she had not experienced with me in years … miracle number three. *Stop*

That Sunday, I prepared myself mentally to attend the church services. Phyllis was more excited than I was. God had allowed great, unknown expectations to embrace us all. We met smiling people on our way to seats near the front. We took up one bench, and I sat at the aisle end. The service began with prayer and scripture readings and something I had not experienced in years, the anointed praise and worship service. The lyrics of the songs penetrated my heart and filled me with the presence of heaven. I was not distracted by anything; I was zoned in hook, line, and sinker.

The pastor spoke with such an anointed voice about God and Jesus; I was always waiting anxiously for his next words. He was well versed in the Word and presented it authoritatively. I began to feel that I belonged there. I reflected on my teen years, a time when I encountered God in a country church in Dade City, Florida, and was baptized in the Holy Spirit. The joy of that glorious encounter sprung up in my soul. I had not felt that good since then.

The sermon ended, and the pastor challenged the congregation about salvation. He appealed to all to understand the importance of a relationship with God through Jesus Christ. He invited people to come up and receive Jesus as their personal Lord and Savior, but I sat there listening intently but with no urge to move. I caught Phyllis's and mother's eyes locked on me. Neither said a word, but they knew as I did that my heart was being challenged. Nonetheless, I had decided not to go up. The pastor asked, "Who here has not committed their lives to Jesus? Please raise your hand." I was reluctant, but I did not want to lie in church, so I raised my hand just a bit. The pastor walked over to me. Our eyes connected. In his very demanding Jamaican accent, he said, "You know you should be up there, so go!"

I respected him and complied by slowly walking to the front of the church. I stood there not really knowing what to expect. The pastor stood in front of me and said, "You need Jesus in your life, and I'm going to pray for you."

I do not recall saying anything; everything became intense. The pastor anointed my head with oil, laid his hand on my forehead, and began praying vigorously and intensely. I felt euphoric; it seemed that a heavy weight was being lifted from my body. I collapsed to the floor with tears of jubilation; uncontrollable praises to God flowed from my mouth. I felt such relief. I was weeping tears of joy while moving back and forth on the floor crying out to God and Jesus with thanks and adoration. I felt free, redeemed, and cleansed of all my past sins of evil. I felt that God forgave me for leaving Him for the pleasures of the world. I experienced His love in such a divine way that I could do nothing but praise Him as His presence engulfed me. I began speaking again in tongues, and I sensed God embracing me. My soul was filled with praises and adoration for my Heavenly Father. I was so happy to return home to Him.

My life was redeemed that Sunday; it was not perfect, but it was redeemed by the blood of Jesus, and I was forgiven. What a day of rejoicing! Phyllis and my mother rejoiced with me on that awesome day! My wife got a real husband, my mother got her son back, and I returned to my loving, Heavenly Father—miracle number four.

God had rewarded Phyllis for having endured my confused lifestyle. I will be forever thankful for her faith in God and for never having given up on me. Our marriage has not been perfect, but we know who stepped in and now walks with both of us on this journey of life. God through His Word has been our road map. Phyllis and I know that our marriage is sacred to God and that we must work to keep it that way. Conflicts will occur, but they will not rule or marriage unless we give them permission to do so, and that will not happen!

I challenge you to honor your spouse as a divine gift from God and be a good steward of God's gift; He is lovingly sharing with you your spouse. Conflicts can get out of control only when you fuel them with selfishness, so take a step back and look within yourself and honestly assess what you are doing to fuel the conflict and stop it! No more conflict. May God bless your marriage with His divine peace and happiness so that it will be a witness of God's love to others.

Living in obedience to God's divine truths is the way to overcome marital challenges. It is God's will that all marriages last and be living witnesses to His love and grace. We need lasting, righteous, and holy marriages to raise like-kind children for the good of our world. Too many marriages fail because of broken unions with God. He is the architect of marriage, which means it is associated with Him and is good.

Husband and wife must comply with God's instructions on how to make holy matrimony work. The directions are simple—Love God first with all of your being and love yourself out of God's love for you; only then can you love your spouse and others. Marriage is etched in the foundation of God's love. The deeper your love grows for God, the deeper it will grow for yourself and your spouse. If you are married, your love life for God will translate into your love life for your spouse and others.

I invite you to read the scripture index for this chapter.

What are your thoughts about the punishment placed on the woman because of her sin? How has it impacted your life story? If you are married, how do you assess your marriage? What miracles have you experienced from God on your journey to eternity?

stop

CHAPTER 17

The Punishment of Man

And to the man he said, "Since you listened to your wife and ate from the tree whose fruit I commanded you not to eat, the ground is cursed because of you. All your life you will struggle to scratch a living from it. It will grow thorns and thistles for you, though you will eat of its grains. By the sweat of your brow will you have food to eat until you return to the ground from which you were made. For you were made from dust, and to dust you will return." (Genesis 3:17–19)

God thus punished Adam for his rebellion in the garden. "Since you listened to your wife …" was the foundation of his indictment. This statement appears to indicate that he had willingly complied with his wife's instructions to eat the fruit without challenging her request.

It is not clear what the mental state of the man was prior to being instructed to eat the fruit since the serpent had not deceived him directly, but we can infer that she convinced him in the same manner she was convinced—by lying to him. He had chosen to eat the fruit in spite of the fact that God had told him not to.

We should never allow anyone to persuade us to sin against God under any circumstances. We should challenge anyone who tries to challenge our hearts to sin because sins are impossible to undo once they are committed. When we disobey God at the behest of another, we place that person ahead of God.

The punishment was severe because it included the dysfunction of other systems: The ground was cursed. The man would face a lifelong struggle with thorns and thistles growing among the grain. He would sweat to produce the food he needed. Food production has become easier due to modern harvesting techniques and equipment, but we still have to contend with insects and plant diseases, and that requires labor and laborers, and the machinery is expensive. The curse on the ground is a devastating struggle for humans.

Assess the consequences to yourself and others pro and con before you make any major decision. I like to commune with God about my future decisions to be assured that I am honoring Him by seeking His guidance. When I feel peace about a matter in my spirit, I act upon it; if I have the slightest bit of uncertainty, I back off and continue seeking directions from God. Whenever I fail to wait on God for direction, I always come up short. When I wait to hear from Him before moving forward and feeling affirmed by His peace, things always work out for my good.

As children of God must know how much God cares for us; we honor Him when we include Him and Jesus in everything we do, including daily matters as well as spiritual matters. When I was new to the faith, I wondered why mature saints would say, "I need to pray about a matter," before they acted. I thought that was over spiritualizing if that were possible. But after a few years of bouncing off the walls of failure after making the wrong decisions, I realized how much I needed to include God in every aspect of my life.

I do not feel comfortable engaging in anything without seeking His guidance. I feel I dishonor God when I make decisions without running them past Him. It is an awesome feeling to have a one-on-one relationship with God that allows me to take everything to Him knowing He cares about me and will make everything work out for my good.

Establish communication timeouts with God, Jesus, and the Holy Spirit apart from your prayer times. They are really great faith builders, and you will get to know them better and better. There are no boundaries to the grace of God. Do not follow the path of our first parents by erecting a self-inflicted boundary between you and God. Always include God in every aspect of your life before you act. It is always better to approach Him for advice and directions rather than to approach Him for forgiveness when you missed the mark because you excluded Him. Before you commit to anything, seek an audience with the Godhead first.

How has the punishment of the man impacted your life? What are you doing to build a trusting relationship with God, and can you improve it?

CHAPTER 18

Banished from the Garden

The latter part of Genesis 3:19 is what I consider the judgment blow for the tragic sin of disobeying the Lord God: "… until you return to the ground from which you were made. For you were made from dust, and to dust you will return." This is true justice carried out by the righteous and just judge, the Lord God. It is true justice because God stays true to His commands; He cannot lie because He has no favorites or reasons to.

> The LORD God placed the man in the Garden of Eden to tend and watch over it. But the LORD God warned him, "You may freely eat the fruit of every tree in the garden— except the tree of the knowledge of good and evil. If you eat its fruit, you are sure to die." (Genesis 2:15–17)

The powerful words *you are sure to die* were imputed on all humankind throughout the ages. Prior to the sin of man, he was destined to live forever. The judgment of death returned the natural man back to the dust from which he was created, and the soul of man goes to either paradise (heaven) or hell (the holding cell) awaiting the Last Judgment.

In Genesis 3:23, God's banishment of humankind from the garden denoted the spiritual death of humankind—separation from God—and its physical death, its return to the dust. Spiritual death occurs when man is banished from God's presence because of sin; God cannot dwell in a sinful body. Our physical deaths occur at different times, but we are spiritually dead from birth; we inherit both deaths because of Adam's and Eve's sin of rebellion. The only way the spirit can regain life is through being born again, as stated in 1 John 1:9 (KJV), "If we confess our sins, he is faithful and just to forgive us our sins, and to cleanse us from all unrighteousness."

The following two verses sum up the devastation caused by the catastrophe in the garden, where the battle started but also where victory was birthed.

> Man *that is* born of a woman *is* of few days, and full of trouble. (Job 14:1 KJV)

> And just as each person is destined to die once and after that comes judgment. (Hebrews 9:27)

Genesis 3:20–24 deals with the exit from the garden of Eden.

> Then the man—Adam—named his wife Eve, because she would be the mother of all who live. And the LORD God made clothing from animal skins for Adam and his wife. Then the LORD God said, "Look, the human beings have become like us, knowing both good and evil. What if they reach out, take fruit from the tree of life, and eat it? Then they will live forever!" So the LORD God banished them from the Garden of Eden, and he sent Adam out to cultivate the ground from which he had been made. After sending them out, the LORD God stationed mighty cherubim to the east of the Garden of Eden. And he placed a flaming sword that flashed back and forth to guard the way to the tree of life.

These verses reveal the true nature of a loving Father who operates out of his loving-kindness and compassion for His creation. Even after they walked away from Him, he displayed His love by clothing them with animal skin; the first recorded death of a living creature, to cover their nakedness, an action never performed before.

Our first parents left the garden with name identification, which added value to their tumultuous existence. God stated they had become like "us," the Godhead, knowing both good and evil. This is a vital point God made. Man would no longer walk solely in the life and environment of perfection and goodness only and function in righteousness and holiness. After eating the fruit, he became knowledgeable of evil as well as good. They had functioned under the system of good, but their sin introduced another system—that of evil. The two systems compete for the control of the soul of humankind through their hearts.

The apostle Paul helps us understand this dilemma in Romans 7:14–15.

> So the trouble is not with the law, for it is spiritual and good. The trouble is with me, for I am all too human, a slave to sin. I don't really understand myself, for I want to do what is right, but I don't do it. Instead, I do what I hate.

This narrative caused my heart to cry out for all humanity because I too can identify with the warfare going on in me between good and evil. My resolve is always in Jesus Christ, the author and finisher of my faith, the reason I hunger to share Jesus Christ with all humanity. He is the antidote to death, the only hope for humanity. Jesus is the good news, the only one by whom humanity can be restored to its rightful relationship with God as His children. Jesus is the only answer for humanity since the catastrophe in the garden.

God banished Adam and Eve from the garden of Eden to prevent them from eating the fruit of the tree of life; that resulted in humans living as outcast from God./ Banishment resulted in humankind tragically being separated from God—suffering spiritual death along with facing the certainty of physical death. We see it lived out today and the mass confusion of evil it is causing.

If you desire to know if good or evil is controlling you, pay attention to the fruit you are producing from your lifestyle. Meditate on the following verses, an enlightening education of what each of us has to endure on our journey to eternal life and the only source of victory—Jesus.

> The sinful nature wants to do evil, which is just the opposite of what the Spirit wants. And the Spirit gives us desires

that are the opposite of what the sinful nature desires. These two forces are constantly fighting each other, so you are not free to carry out your good intentions. (Galatians 5:17)

So the trouble is not with the law, for it is spiritual and good. The trouble is with me, for I am all too human, a slave to sin. I don't really understand myself, for I want to do what is right, but I don't do it. Instead, I do what I hate. But if I know that what I am doing is wrong, this shows that I agree that the law is good. So I am not the one doing wrong; it is sin living in me that does it. And I know that nothing good lives in me, that is, in my sinful nature. I want to do what is right, but I can't. I want to do what is good, but I don't. I don't want to do what is wrong, but I do it anyway. But if I do what I don't want to do, I am not really the one doing wrong; it is sin living in me that does it. I have discovered this principle of life—that when I want to do what is right, I inevitably do what is wrong. I love God's law with all my heart. But there is another power within me that is at war with my mind. This power makes me a slave to the sin that is still within me. Oh, what a miserable person I am! Who will free me from this life that is dominated by sin and death? Thank God! The answer is in Jesus Christ our Lord. So you see how it is: In my mind I really want to obey God's law, but because of my sinful nature I am a slave to sin. (Romans 7:14–25)

This is a crucial teaching for all humanity and the way to overcome the evils that are tearing humankind apart. We must learn from our first parents and the truths given to us by God so we can walk in harmony with God again.

Satan seeks to have you spend eternity with him in the Lake of Fire forever with no hope of deliverance, while God seeks to have you spend eternity with Him on the new earth in your new, glorified body in fellowship with Him again. Either evil or good will lead you to your eternal destiny. The life you are living is telling your story and mapping out your eternal future. I challenge you to monitor your daily journey by setting your soul compass on Jesus Christ so that your mind will focus on Him; your fruit will reflect your heart.

Evil has no conscience; it causes hatred and uncontrollable behavior, and it causes us to see fellow humans as our enemies who must be destroyed. Satan's mission is to kill, steal, and destroy all humans because we are all made in God's image. He hates God because he could not overthrow Him; therefore, he attacks what is associated with God and in particular His prized creation, humankind. It is spiritual warfare perpetrated by Satan against God and His creation.

Humanity has been Satan's target since Adam and Eve; he caused them to rebel against God and denounce Him through their sinister actions.

Good and evil are the initiators of spiritual warfare for the souls of humanity. Satan steals, kills, and destroys, the trinity of evil, but God offers us faith, hope, and love, the trinity of good.

> The thief's purpose is to steal and kill and destroy. (John 10:10)

> Three things will last forever—faith, hope, and love—and the greatest of these is love. (1 Corinthians 13:13)

What are your thoughts about the banishment of humanity from the presence of God? Have you ever experienced a void, an absence of God, in your soul? What fruits are you currently producing that do not represent God in your life?

CHAPTER 19

That None Perish!

We must realize that we are Satan's targets. We cannot allow him to continue to operate incognito resulting in the destruction of fellow humans. Everyone is important, and everyone is significant, and everyone is a blessing. God's heartbeat must be the heartbeat of every child of His. Let's learn from Him and capture His heart for all humanity as presented in 2 Peter 3:9 (NKJV): "The Lord is not slack concerning His promise, as some count slackness, but is longsuffering toward us, not willing that any should perish but that all should come to repentance."

God desires all to be saved from eternal damnation; He is so committed to the cause that He gave His only begotten Son …

> … that whoever believes in Him should not perish but have eternal life. For God so loved the world that He gave His only begotten Son, that whoever believes in Him should not perish but have everlasting life. For God did not send His Son into the world to condemn the world, but that the world through Him might be saved. (John 3:15–17 NKJV)

We have established that God's supernatural plan of salvation was birthed out of the fall of our first parents and for the demise of His longtime nemesis, Satan, and his minions. The plan of salvation is the restrainer holding back the return of Jesus because God "is willing that none perish." His true church has His heart and has embraced His wish that none perish. We must fulfill the Great Commission Jesus gave us in Matthew 28:18–20.

stop

> Jesus came and told his disciples, "I have been given all authority in heaven and on earth. Therefore, go and make disciples of all the nations, baptizing them in the name of the Father and the Son and the Holy Spirit. Teach these new disciples to obey all the commands I have given you. And be sure of this: I am with you always, even to the end of the age." We have the heart of God in our souls; but what about those who are perishing? God's love for them compels us to practice the ministry of reconciliation so that none will perish. And all of this is a gift from God, who brought us back to himself through Christ. And God has given us this task of reconciling people to him. For God was in Christ, reconciling the world to himself, no longer counting people's sins against them. And he gave us this wonderful message of reconciliation. So we are Christ's ambassadors; God is making his appeal through us. We speak for Christ when we plead, "Come back to God!" For God made Christ, who never sinned, to be the offering for our sin, so that we could be made right with God through Christ. (2 Corinthians 5:18–21)

I challenge you to make your life count by sharing Jesus with those who are perishing. Get into the war for souls and become God's difference maker for the good of humanity and His glory!

We must prepare to battle Satan every second of our lives because we value souls as our Heavenly Father does. The apostle Paul was one of our elite warriors and leaders, so let us focus on what he advised for this type of warfare in Ephesians 6:11:11–12.

> Put on all of God's armor so that you will be able to stand firm against all strategies of the devil. For we are not

fighting against flesh-and-blood enemies, but against evil
rulers and authorities of the unseen world, against mighty
powers in this dark world, and against evil spirits in the
heavenly places.

This is strategic information for our battle for souls that are perishing
at the hands of Satan, the world and the flesh. The Word of God states
that one of the major weaknesses on our journey to eternity is a lack of
knowledge. Knowledge implies that we are informed about the endeavor
or assignment we will engage in. Without that knowledge, we are at a
disadvantage and face defeat. Even if it means researching, studying,
and assessing the situation, we should gain the knowledge we need to
accomplish the call of God on our lives. Preparation is 90 percent of
success. The apostle Paul identified our enemies and what we need to defeat
them … What a blessing! If we comply with his instructions, we will be
more than conquerors.

Our failure to act on this crucial information has given Satan and
advantage over the church. Rather than fighting our real enemies, we
fight one another because we have been duped into believing our enemies
are our fellow human beings and recruiting others to attack one another.
These actions lead to divisions and hatred causing the church to become
dysfunctional.

As stated previously, the apostle Paul identified the real enemy to all
humanity—the lies that other ethnic groups or individuals are out to
destroy us and that we must defend ourselves; satanic lies that provoke fear
and confusion are the cause of all wars. Ephesians 6:10–12 reads,

> For we are not fighting against flesh-and-blood enemies,
> but against evil rulers and authorities of the unseen world,
> against mighty powers in this dark world, and against evil
> spirits in the heavenly places.

We must overcome evil by doing good so that no one will be defeated
by evil as our first parents and those who have missed the freedom provided
by God through His Son, Jesus.

God's truths have revealed the evil workings of the sinful mind and the righteous workings of the spirit mind. Let's focus on the truth of God's Word so we can recognize and denounce evil and take hold of goodness and live. We must strive for unity with one another by recognizing that everyone is important and significant and a blessing to each other. Let's practice lifting up one another rather than demeaning one another. We are beautiful when we honor God by loving one another. The truth teaches us how to think and live to prevent the knowledge of evil from controlling us.

Meditate on the truths of God daily so your life story will end forever in His presence and you will hear Him say, "Well done my good and faithful servant enter into my eternal rest and reign with me forever and ever!" (Matthew 25:21 KJV). Amen and amen!

God created you to receive you into His kingdom and be with Him forever. Do not allow Satan to deceive you by stealing your love for God, yourself and fellow humans and replacing it with hatred!

How have acts of hatred impacted your life? Have you discovered the joy of encouraging others daily? How do you feel when someone lifts you up and encourage you to do good? How do you feel when lifting others up and encouraging them to do good? I invite you to please review the scripture index page for this chapter.

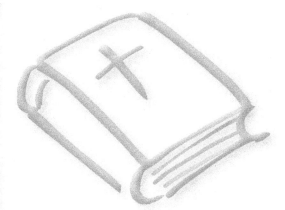

CHAPTER 20

God's Supernatural Plan of Salvation

God's truths have been the key to my born-again transformation. Please read these truths if you desire eternal life with Him.

> And we know that God causes everything to work together for the good of those who love God and are called according to his purpose for them. For God knew his people in advance, and he chose them to become like his Son, so that his Son would be the firstborn among many brothers and sisters. And having chosen them, he called them to come to him. And having called them, he gave them right standing with himself. And having given them right standing, he gave them his glory. (Romans 8:28–30)

God once again opened up His architectural design in a new makeover, this time, His prized trophy, humankind. After the catastrophe in the garden, God planned to deal with Satan and his followers once and for all.

Before we focus on God's plan of salvation, let's explore how God will end Satan's reign of evil.

Then the devil, who had deceived them, was thrown into the fiery lake of burning sulfur, joining the beast and the false prophet. There they will be tormented day and night forever and ever. And anyone whose name was not found recorded in the Book of Life was thrown into the lake of fire. (Revelation 20:10,15)

This assures us that a day of doom is awaiting Satan and his followers, glorious news for the children of God, who will escape eternal damnation in the Lake of Fire, which was created for Satan and those who rejected God's plan of salvation. He will cast Satan into the Lake of Fire, Satan's eternal place of incarceration that will include painful punishment. This is the first essential action God will take to secure salvation for those who follow Jesus Christ. God's plan of salvation provides the only pathway for the righteous and holy to escape eternal damnation and enjoy eternal life with Him.

Humankind has been in a state of dysfunction and chaos because of Satan's deceptions. The world has become a cesspool of sin—everyone doing what is right in their own eyes. The first murder was committed by a child of our first parents; since then, sin consumed the earth causing God to destroy it by a worldwide deluge in which all but eight perished—Noah and his family. God raised the Israelites under the leadership of Abraham to be a light of hope for other heathen nations, but the Israelites rebelled against Abraham and God. God, however, did not give up on them; He gave them Moses and the Ten Commandments. The Israelites followed the path of our first parents and rebelled against God continuously. After many other leaders, they continued to rebel against God until God withdrew from humankind for four hundred years due to their evilness. The world continues to live in sin choosing evil over good.

Because God's truths enlighten and warn us of what is taking place and will take place before the end of the world, we must comprehend them. These warnings are to prepare us for Jesus's return and the coming of God's new heavens and earth. How are we to prepare for another new world under God? God has made the answer simple under His plan of salvation; He announced in Genesis 3:15 that Jesus was the seed of the woman He promised to destroy Satan's reign of evil and terror against

Him. To experience God's plan of salvation, the following truths have to be fulfilled.

When our first parents were banned from the garden, they were also removed from fellowship with God. They were punished with physical death and separation from God, which resulted in their spiritual deaths as well. God designed a path for the spirit system of humans to be born again so He could reestablish His loving fellowship with them. What a loving, Heavenly Father; He gave us a second chance! Let's embrace His awesome plan of salvation, which He designed to rescue us from the world, the flesh, and the devil.

His plan empowers us to endure and escape the dysfunctional world, its demise, and its evil systems resulting from the catastrophe in the garden. We live in the world, but the world systems cannot control children of God when they live in compliance with God's plan. We will suffer, be tempted, and be persecuted in this evil world, but under God's plan, we will endure and receive eternal life with Him. (Please read the supporting scriptures in the scripture index for this chapter.)

To create His plan of salvation, He returned to His architectural makeover skills He displayed in the creation phase. He redesigned the human system to become a unified structure so human beings would honor and worship Him once again. God maintains His divine righteousness and holiness. His indwelling Holy Spirit becomes His operational system that works with the spirit system of humans. They join to form His holistic structure known as His church, which comprises its many members working together, the born-again children of God. Their functions are defined by His truths, which His Holy Spirit, angelic messengers, and gifted servants deliver individually or collectively.

The church is God's structure designed to worship and honor Him and perform the work of the ministry of reconciliation. The church consists of born-again children of God who worship Him in spirit and in truth under the anointing of the indwelling Holy Spirit. They are empowered by the Holy Spirit to become witnesses of Jesus Christ, who rescues the lost from eternal damnation.

Christians must share Jesus, the good news, with humankind for their salvation. He is God's sacrificial gift for the salvation of humankind. God gave His Son so that none would perish, and He gave His church the task of spreading the good news (Jesus), so that none would perish. God, His Holy Spirit, God's chief administrator of His church, and Jesus, its head, have no favorites. There is no need of competition for God's love, it is unlimited and flows freely to all who desires to receive it.

Let's explore how God's plan of salvation transforms dysfunctional people into His obedient children. A transformed life is a born-again life. In John 3:3, 5–6, Jesus stated,

> I tell you the truth, unless you are born again, you cannot see the Kingdom of God … I assure you; no one can enter the Kingdom of God without being born of water and the Spirit. Humans can reproduce only human life, but the Holy Spirit gives birth to spiritual life.

1 Peter 1:23–25, states,

> For you have been born again, but not to a life that will quickly end. Your new life will last forever because it comes from the eternal, living word of God. As the Scriptures say, "People are like grass; their beauty is like a flower in the field. The grass withers and the flower fades. But the word of the Lord remains forever." And that word is the Good News that was preached to you.

Becoming born again requires three actions; the first is to confess Jesus as your Lord and Savior as stated in Romans 10:9–10.

> If you confess with your mouth that Jesus is Lord and believe in your heart that God raised him from the dead, you will be saved. For it is by believing in your heart that you are made right with God, and it is by confessing with your mouth that you are saved.

The second is water baptism—being submerged in water.

> After his baptism, as Jesus came up out of the water, the heavens were opened and he saw the Spirit of God

descending like a dove and settling on him. (Matthew 3:16)

Stop Well then, should we keep on sinning so that God can show us more and more of his wonderful grace? Of course not! Since we have died to sin, how can we continue to live in it? Or have you forgotten that when we were joined with Christ Jesus in baptism, we joined him in his death? For we died and were buried with Christ by baptism. And just as Christ was raised from the dead by the glorious power of the Father, now we also may live new lives. Since we have been united with him in his death, we will also be raised to life as he was. We know that our old sinful selves were crucified with Christ so that sin might lose its power in our lives. We are no longer slaves to sin. For when we died with Christ we were set free from the power of sin. And since we died with Christ, we know we will also live with him. We are sure of this because Christ was raised from the dead, and he will never die again. Death no longer has any power over him. When he died, he died once to break the power of sin. But now that he lives, he lives for the glory of God. So you also should consider yourselves to be dead to the power of sin and alive to God through Christ Jesus. (Romans 6:1–11)

Baptism symbolizes the death, burial, and resurrection of Jesus Christ; the baptized are witnesses to the world that they were baptized unto Jesus Christ and have become one with Him. Leaving the ways of the world and entering a life in Jesus glorifies God.

The third act is baptism in the Holy Spirit. Spirit baptism is inviting the Holy Spirit to take up residence into one's soul. This act of baptism along with the other two acts completes the born-again process, which is necessary for human transformation through God's salvation plan. The born-again experience produces the human-spiritual structure that is required by God to bring honor and glory to Him and His Godhead. The spiritual life replicates the heart and nature of God, which is manifested through living a righteous holy obedient life of love unto God while living in this present evil world.

Jesus taught the significance of being born again in John 3:3–7 (KJV).

> Verily, verily, I say unto thee, Except a man be born again, he cannot see the kingdom of God. Nicodemus saith unto him, How can a man be born when he is old? can he enter the second time into his mother's womb, and be born? Jesus answered, Verily, verily, I say unto thee, Except a man be born of water and *of* the Spirit, he cannot enter into the kingdom of God. That which is born of the flesh is flesh; and that which is born of the Spirit is spirit. Marvel not that I said unto thee, Ye must be born again.

Holy Spirit baptism is known to take place either prior to or after water baptism; no order is designated.

God's transformational plan of salvation consists of four steps that constitute the born-again experience. ***The first step in God's transformational plan of salvation is acknowledging and honoring the presence of the Holy Spirit.*** Please review the scriptures in the scripture index for this chapter; they reveal God's truth, the only way for true transformation to occur. The awesome born-again experience is a divine transformation by God through the faith of His children. When the Holy Spirit is invited to dwell in the child of God, a supernatural hereditary transformation ensues; the Holy Spirit infuses dead spirits with God's DNA, and those spirits inherit God's divine nature and character bringing them to life. We must realize that we are God's vessels of love, righteousness, and holiness made possible by the fruit of the Spirit in Galatians 5:22–23, which is produced by the indwelling Holy Spirit. We do not have to pretend to love others or pretend to produce order and moral conduct; that is who we are when we allow the Holy Spirit to guide our lives. As children of God, we live it; it is our new DNA. Spiritual death is resolved when we return to God through the born-again experience and our future inheritance is guaranteed by the indwelling Holy Spirit. I encourage you to follow the lead of the Holy Spirit and he will transform you.

In Luke 11:13, Jesus said, "So if you sinful people know how to give good gifts to your children, how much more will your Heavenly Father give the Holy Spirit to those who ask him."

The second step in God's transformational plan of salvation is receiving your new identity. Under God's method of operation, function determines the identity and composition of the structure and the desired outcome shapes the function. Therefore, our true identity based on function is that of children of God. Our known identity dictates our functional purpose.

> And we know that God causes everything to work together for the good of those who love God and are called according to his purpose for them. For God knew his people in advance, and he chose them to become like his Son, so that his Son would be the firstborn among many brothers and sisters. (Romans 8:28–30)

The above passage lays out God's system for transforming those who love Him into the likeness of His Son and makes them His children. God has to be acknowledged as our Heavenly Father whom we honor and glorify. We must be proud to be identified as God's born-again children purchased by the blood of our elder brother, Jesus Christ.

When you acknowledge God as your Heavenly Father, you will respect and honor Him as such. He is an awesome Father who provides for His children. Renew your mind by acknowledging your personal relationship with God, your Heavenly Father, Jesus, your elder brother and friend, and the Holy Spirit, your personal comforter and teacher. Walk in your true identity as a born-again child of God or forever search for your identity in all the wrong places. Your confident assurance is crucial for taking the next step in your transformation.

This step is very challenging for those who are excited about their newfound relationship with God; they can be driven by their emotions rather than the guidance of the Holy Spirit. I know; this is where I missed the mark on my first pursuit of God when I was a teen. After a short time, the emotions and excitement abates and people learn they are not as saved and committed as first thought.

The transformation journey includes discipleship, a crucial process, the essential introduction to your complete transformation. Without divine discipleship, you become like a gorgeous potted plant that starts with a glowing promise of continued beauty and great possibilities but withers without the sustaining provision of water. I challenge you not to take the path of the potted plant but seek and demand sustaining divine discipleship.

Discipleship is a crucial training period that requires a mentor or coach to walk with you through the early infancy of your born-again experience and beyond. The time that takes is different for everyone. As a new babe in Christ, you will spend an inordinate amount of time in prayer, fasting, and studying the Word on your own and with your mentors. Churches usually have a discipleship plan for converts to help them develop the nature and character of God as their way of life.

We cannot afford to have people fall off or give up on this awesome transformation journey by not equipping them to live under the leadership of the Holy Spirit; their eternal lives are at stake. Pray for God through the leading of the Holy Spirit to assign you a brother or sister who replicates Jesus rather than self-serving individuals trying to build their kingdom at your expense.

As born-again children of God must become who God says we are for His honor and glory, not ours or anyone else's. Inheriting eternal life has to be our desired outcome above all else. We are spiritually transformed when our minds are consumed with the knowledge and ways of God through Jesus Christ achieved through studying and allowing His truths to become our way of life.

Let everything you do reflect your loving relationship with your Heavenly Father. Do what you see Him doing and join Him; that is the advice of your elder brother, Jesus. Meditate on the promises your Father has given you and allow them to become your desired outcome for your own good and His glory.

The Holy Spirit is your teacher who will lead you through your transformation process; that is one of His functions while yours is to submit to and follow Him instead of rejecting Him. The Holy Spirit is your advocate from God who dwells in you to teach you to live a life that honors and glorifies God. He is your built-in GPS system to eternal life. He is also your security system teaching you to produce good and avoid evil. The

Holy Spirit is so significant in the Godhead that any act of blaspheming, speaking against, insulting, or cursing Him comes with dire consequences and no forgiveness. Please cherish and respect His presence in your life; He is your seal of God's ownership.

Acknowledging your true identity as a child of God will transform everything about you. Your life will be a living reflection of God's divine nature resulting in your being one with your Heavenly Father. I cannot express the value added through my daily communications with Him, Jesus, and the Holy Spirit; they are my source of enduring joy.

The way to know God is through studying and meditating on His truths, which will feed your spirit continuously along with prayer vigils, and hearing God's Word preached and taught by gifted servants. When you are a born-again child of God, your spirit will hunger to be in continuous fellowship with the Godhead. Attach yourself to the Holy Spirit and follow His lead and you will not regret it. Do all things to please our Heavenly Father; you will never be forsaken or defeated when you allow the Godhead to dwell in you because you will possess all you need to be complete.

The third step in God's transformational plan of salvation is loving and obeying God. We cannot accomplish this step without fulfilling the first two steps. It is essential that we are secure in our born-again spirits and be sure that we are born-again children of God and function as one. We will know by the transformation in our lives and the fruit we produce. The Holy Spirit dwelling in us will provide the confident assurance that we are indeed His children.

Faith, hope, and love, the trinity of good, are foundational in fulfilling the third step of loving and obeying God. 1 Corinthians 13:13 (NLT), states, "Three things will last forever—faith, hope, and love—and the greatest of these is love." Good is who God is and what He requires of humanity. Only God can define and receive what is good. As we learned earlier, good is God's personal expression of approval. God's acknowledgement of good is the standard of approval one should desire to hear expressed by God on one's behalf. "Thy good and faithful servant enter into my rest" (Matthew 25:21) is the acceptance response all children of God look forward to hearing from Him. Therefore, we must master faith, hope, and love if we expect to be transformed into the likeness of Jesus Christ, our example.

Faith, the first word of the trinity of good, is defined in Hebrews 11:1:

"Faith is the confidence that what we hope for will actually happen; it gives us assurance about things we cannot see." That verse provides a road map of how faith must be allowed to manifest itself in the child of God. Faith is simply undeterred trust and belief in God through love for Him fulfilled by obediently living out His truths without reservation. Living a life of faith, adhering to the truths of God, is key to pleasing Him. Faith allows us to say, "I am God's child, and whatever His will is for my life is my will for His glory." (Please study the scriptures on faith in the scripture index for this chapter.)

Hope, the second word of the trinity of good, is expressed in Romans 8:23–25.

> And we believers also groan, even though we have the Holy Spirit within us as a foretaste of future glory, for we long for our bodies to be released from sin and suffering. We, too, wait with eager hope for the day when God will give us our full rights as his adopted children, including the new bodies he has promised us. We were given this hope when we were saved. (If we already have something, we don't need to hope for it. But if we look forward to something we don't yet have, we must wait patiently and confidently.)

Hope inspires in us a deep anticipation for a desired outcome. Our hope is based on the great and precious promises He gave us. Hope generates and builds our assurance as we wait patiently for the promises to be fulfilled. Hope allows us to dream of what life will be like in the future.

The greatest advantage to living a life full of hope is its power to position you to inherit God's promises. If the promise of eternal life is not inspiring you, assess your true eternal future with God or Satan. I know which one will win out, so embrace your hope and pursue it relentlessly on your journey to eternal life.

Love, the third word of the trinity of good, is defined in *The Practical Word Study of The New Testament.*

God is love; He is full of love (*agapē*): a selfless and sacrificial love; a love of the mind, of the reason, of the will as well as of the heart and affections.

It is the love that goes so far ... that it loves a person even if he does not deserve to be loved, that it loves the person who is utterly unworthy of being loved, that it is compelled to sacrifice itself for its enemies.2

Agape love originates with God as do all the attributes of goodness. God is good because He personifies love, which everything in the universe displays. All of creation is birthed out of God's divine nature of love. Love is the greatest revelation to humankind of who God is. It is the only word that can accurately describe, define, and identify Him. Love is all God is and is the foundation of all His actions. God moves and has His being through love. God's love is the bond of His perfection from which flows His joy, peace, patience, kindness, goodness, faithfulness, gentleness, and long-suffering engulfed by His righteousness and holiness!

God pours out His love into the hearts of all who acknowledge Him as their Heavenly Father through their born-again transformation. We possess the nature of God through His Spirit, which dwells in each of us. God is requiring all His children to become like His son. He does not force us but desires each of us to surrender to Him with our free will because of the unlimited love He *2. Leadership Ministries Worldwide. (2004). Practical Word Studies in The New Testament, Page; 1291, L-#2432: Love; Loved.*

provides to us. He showcased His love by creating humankind in His image and likeness for the sake of fellowship with them; He gave His Son as a living sacrifice to rescue all humanity from eternal damnation and to forever be with Him. He fills every child with the Holy Spirit as His personal seal of ownership.

The Holy Spirit imparts God's nature into our souls enabling us to function according to God's perfect will for His glory and the good of humanity. As if that were not enough, He has provided us with eternal life to encourage and motivate us to eagerly embrace Him and His ways with our overflowing love for the Godhead and one another.

The significant value love plays in God's plan of salvation has to resonate in the heart of every child of God as an absolute mandate. Without love, you will never know or experience God, but you will tragically secure your eternal destiny in the Lake of Fire. When questioned in Matthew 19:16, "Teacher, what good deed must I do to have eternal life?" Jesus responded in verse 17, "... if you want to receive eternal life, keep the commandments." Later in Matthew 22:35, Jesus was asked, "Which is the most important commandment in the law of Moses?" Jesus responded in verses 36–40,

> "You must love the LORD your God with all your heart, all your soul, and all your mind." This is the first and greatest commandment. A second is equally important: "Love your neighbor as yourself." The entire law and all the demands of the prophets are based on these two commandments.

Jesus confirmed the key takeaway from the above narrative—eternal life is secured by obeying God's greatest commandments anchored in love, His truths. Since evil was imputed on all humanity, the key antidote for overcoming evil is allowing the love for God to be shared with one another, which brings out the good in us all. Love is the purification system placed in the hearts of all God's children to filter out any and everything anti-God! Therefore, allow agape love to be the foundation of your life evidenced in all you do to assure your inheritance of eternal life. You got this!

We have completed our discussion on the trinity of good. The three divine functional transformational virtues imparted into the life of born-again children of God by the Holy Spirit. Let's refocus on the third step in the transformation process—loving and obeying God. When you are a child of God, love is your greatest virtue for living a victorious life of righteousness and holiness unto God. Love is also your greatest weapon in your warfare against evil. Spiritual warfare takes place here on earth and in this life. Satan will attempt to deceive, slander, and destroy you in an attempt to stop you from exposing him and his evilness. Therefore, as shared earlier, the truths of God are your weapons of victory through love.

God's plan of salvation is awesome because it is birthed out of His love for His creation. Our obedient love for God manifests our faithfulness to Him and results in all things working together for our good. As we continue loving and embracing God's truths, our election and calling remain secure in Jesus.

The human transformation is achieved by loving and obeying God's truths. Love is God's glue that holds the human being together as His unified, functional structure for good. Love is the protective covering for every born-again child of God.

Know with confident assurance that you are God's transformed love child destined to make a difference for the good of all humanity.

> Above all, clothe yourselves with love, which binds us all together in perfect harmony. (Colossians 3:14)

> Most important of all, continue to show deep love for each other, for love covers a multitude of sins. (1 Peter 4:8)

The fourth and final step in God's transformational plan of salvation is becoming focused on your desired outcome—gaining eternal life. When you focus on your future, you become a functional visionary. Focusing requires you to center your heart on this target by concentrating all your effort toward your desired outcome. It takes mental and physical energy to maintain a continuous focus while waiting patiently for your desired outcome to arrive.

Being active mentally and physically in achieving your desired outcome requires committed and endless sacrificing. Studying, meditating, and communing with God the Father, God the Son, and God the Holy Spirit in prayer demand self-discipline and heart-driven dedication. Future-focused children of God are energized warriors who stay focused and battle-ready while pursuing their eternal rewards because the trinity of evil is attempting to steal their faith, kill their hope, and destroy their love.

Future-focusing is one of the most powerful motivating tools a person must possess and cherish. The desired outcome must be continuously managed and systematically fed to the heart and mind. The desired outcome has to resonate in your mind and play out in your soul through divine thoughts and imaginations; it has to consume your will.

Your mind will reveal when your soul has been transformed by God's truths. The transformation of the soul is accomplished by renewing the mind with God's Word and being fruitfully practiced in the life of the child of God for all to see. Your testimony will become as the apostle Paul's did in Galatians 2:20: "My old self has been crucified with Christ. It is no longer I who live, but Christ lives in me. So I live in this earthly body by trusting in the Son of God, who loved me and gave himself for me."

When Jesus becomes the central focus of trust in your life and your life shadows His life, you will receive the gift of eternal life, which has to be the cherished, desired outcome for all who believe in God. It means a transformed and glorified body designed to inhabit a new cosmos and earth and to be in unity with the Godhead—no more sins of evilness, sickness, death, disease, and anything else anti-God; only righteousness and holiness wrapped up in love. Whoa! That's what eternal life looks like, amen. Everyone deserves eternal life!

Colossians 3:1–4 highlights this special, life-transforming promise of eternal life.

> Since you have been raised to new life with Christ, set your sights on the realities of heaven, where Christ sits in the place of honor at God's right hand. Think about the things of heaven, not the things of earth. For you died to this life, and your real life is hidden with Christ in God. And when Christ, who is your life, is revealed to the whole world, you will share in all his glory. Amen!

Rejoice with the Apostle Peter as you express the joy of your glorious future with him in 1 Peter 1:3-5.

The Hope of Eternal Life

[3] All praise to God, the Father of our Lord Jesus Christ. It is by his great mercy that we have been born again, because God raised Jesus Christ from the dead. Now we live with great expectation, [4] and we have a priceless inheritance—an inheritance that is kept in heaven for you, pure and undefiled, beyond the reach of change and decay.

What are your thoughts about being a born-again child of God? How will that experience impact your life? Have you started your transformation process by the renewal your mind? What does eternal life mean to you? How has God's love for you impacted your life?

CHAPTER 21

My Story Framed by the Creation Story

The creation story is the most fascinating narrative; it has helped me tremendously in getting to know God and His heart for humankind. He is a God of love and mercy, and His ways are worth finding out. I have served God for over fifty years now, and each year, He has revealed Himself to me through various situations and circumstances that enabled me to learn about Him and His ways. I am a living witness of how He causes all things to work together for my good.

One of my greatest joys is my time of fellowship with the Godhead. It is a time when I feel God's presence and hear His quiet voice instructing me. Those times are worth their weight in gold to me. The journey to eternal life comes with challenges of various types, but I have learned that they are an asset because they drive me to seek refuge in my Heavenly Father.

Writing this book made me realize what a friend and loving, Heavenly Father He is. I often reflect on my challenges of the past and how He in His glorious wisdom was Jehovah Jireh for me. He really provides all we need this side of heaven. My desire for eternal life with God motivates me to do good and seek Him.

I had been living a life absent from God until my wife, Phyllis, was born again while I was away in college. She shared with me her salvation experience, and knowing I had walked away from God during my early teens, she knew I needed to return to God. She challenged me to return to God. I saw an awesome change in her. I was struggling with my life after spending three years in the military, fifteen months of which were in Vietnam. I was wounded in combat on my first tour and felt a need to return for another tour for revenge and to remove the guilt that had consumed me for getting wounded. The return did not remove my guilt. After leaving the military, I became a police officer, and my confused life became more confused.

I grew up in two churches, the one my grandmother attended, the African Methodist Episcopal Church, Mount Zion (Methodist) and the Church of God in Christ (Pentecostal), which my mother attended. I was most active in the Pentecostal church. I was assigned to teach the younger children's Sunday school and an evening class for young people.

My first encounter with God was at age thirteen while attending a revival. In those days, one was truly redeemed by tarrying for the Holy Spirit. (That could be practical today; just a thought.) The first night of the revival, my loving mother persuaded me to go to the altar and tarry for the Holy Spirit. I had seen others tarry but had never fully understood the process.

My experience at the altar was unique. The singing and music began, and so did the tarrying. I kneeled at the altar and was instructed by my mother and the other church mothers to call on Jesus, so I began to call out Jesus's name. After several minutes of tarrying, I felt I was making progress; I felt a desire to receive Jesus. I did not understand what that looked like, but I knew it would bring me great joy based on what I had witnessed happening to others who had tarried.

My saliva foamed in my mouth after the repeated and intense encouragement to call on Jesus with a great desire for Him. I had the mothers patting and rubbing my back, pouring blessed olive oil on my head, and screaming, "Call him, son!" Every so often, one would scream in my ear, "Jesus! Jesus! Jesus!" and that inspired me to do the same.

As the minutes turned into what seemed hours, the saliva foamed and flowed from my mouth, and I tasted blood in my mouth; my arms, hands, and whole body shook uncontrollably. One mother would wipe the saliva from my mouth while continuing to encourage me. Finally, the singing and music lowered, and we were instructed to get up; we were assisted back to the bench and sat. I was soaking wet from the heat and physical exertion since there was no air conditioning in that old, wood building. It was quite an exciting night for a thirteen-year-old. However, I thoroughly enjoyed it and could not wait until the following night.

The added blessing to that time was that the revival continued the next day on my high school campus (Mickens High) with several students. I was blessed to have several juniors and seniors who had been baptized in the Holy Spirit as mentors. We declared that day to be a day of fasting and prayer for the Holy Spirit's outpouring on the campus. We gathered in the adjoining cow pasture for prayer and studying of God's Word. It was awesome! I was so excited that I could not wait for the service that night. I was one fasted and prayed-up young man ready to receive the baptism of the Holy Spirit.

When I look back over my life, it was one of my most exciting and memorable times. I and other seekers arrived at the church early in great anticipation of receiving the Holy Spirit. We all sat in the front pew and waited with great anticipation for the altar call after Pastor Hansberry finished his powerful preaching. While waiting, I thought about the goodness of God. My heart was primed and ready to receive the Holy Spirit.

In reality, I had no idea what to expect. When the call came to go to the altar, I was one of the first there. I started calling on the name of Jesus and felt the same sensations I had experienced the night before. I did not speak in tongues at the altar. At the end of the altar call, the pastor had the seekers stand up, and he asked them one by one, "How do you feel?" I was the fifth person in the row and was very nervous; I did not know how to respond to the question. As he got closer to me, I prayed, *God, please give me something to say!* When the pastor got to me, asked me his question, and pointed the microphone at my mouth, I was prepared to say, "I feel great," but my tongue took over and I spoke in tongues; I was being filled with the Holy Spirit. I could not control my tongue as it continued to spew out unknown languages to me as described in the Bible. I was crying, jumping, and just lost in unexpected spiritual euphoria. The entire congregation was rejoicing with me and over me.

That night was a life-changer for me. For months, I prayed and studied the Word of God. I played church with my brothers, sister, cousin, and friends at home and in a field, and everywhere else I could praise God. One dear friend was a child preacher (Major), Gwen, my younger sister, and my younger brothers Dave, Ronald, and Robert and I would support him when he preached at the labor camp in our community. That was an awesome experience. I enjoyed the fellowship with my high school mentors and others at school. We would even sneak and read the Bible during classes.

Unfortunately, it did not last for me. I was a young teen, and the pleasures of the world overcame me. I held out until my sophomore year of high school, but then, I explored worldly things and enjoyed them, so my time in church was no longer exciting except when I saw the girls and met with my friends. I experienced alcohol just before graduating from high school and got drunk, which began my sad decline into a backslidden life.

When I joined the army, I became a hard-core soldier and a hard-core sinner. I learned to enjoy women, alcohol, marijuana, gambling, and lying with and to my friends about nothing. After being wounded in battle, I knew God was with me because I should have died that awful day, February 25, 1967, on a battlefield in Lam Dong, South Vietnam. God honored the prayers of my mother, Amanda, my grand mom, Parrie Lee, and my older sister, Mary.

The tragedy of the worst day of my life was walking into an enemy ambush and becoming pinned down by gunfire. I was the assistant machine gunner in a firefight that lasted longer and was more intense than most. We were running very low on ammo, so the machine gunner pulled back to protect the command position. I was left alone to hold the position behind a small tree with my rifle, which was jamming after each round I fired. Gunships were called in and began firing rockets on our positions due to the closely engaged fighting. The rockets ignited the underbrush, and it began to burn rapidly with six-foot flames coming directly toward me and between me and my enemies.

When I tried to pull my rucksack and my machine gunner's rucksack out of the path of the brush fire, I was shot in my leg just below the knee and was in a lot of pain. I had been spun around, and I started crawling out of the line of fire. My dear friends Franks and Charles yelled, Shoot!

The VC's are in front of you." I yelled back that I had been hit and that my weapon had jammed.

Franks ran up within ten feet of me and kneeled to fire when the automatic weapon fire that had me pinned down opened up on him. I saw blood flow from his face and chest; his eyes connected with mine, and he appeared to be saying, *Smithy, I'm sorry I can't help you!* He fell. He was motionless. I knew he was dead. I lost sight of Charles.

Doc, the medic, ran to me, but I told him that Franks had been hit several times and that he should check on him first. He noticed that my rucksack, just a few feet away from us, was on fire due to the brush fire. He asked me if any grenades were in it, and I told him yes. He threw his body beside mine and told me to hug the ground. A loud explosion … My hearing and sight were gone … Everything appeared to be a complete whiteout … When my eyesight and hearing returned shortly after the explosion, I realized I was alive, and I refocused. The explosion had impacted several VC, but a piece of shrapnel struck Charles in his head.

When I saw Charles in the field hospital later, he was bleeding and unconscious. I am grateful to God that Charles did not succumb to his wound. Those guys are my heroes.

Frank's death made Jesus's death a reality for me. I saw a friend sacrifice his life helping me. I made it, but my life has been traumatized by that horrible day. My life was confused. Before I repented and returned to the Lord, I was a sinful, wicked soul on my way to hell. I knew my lifestyle was anti-God and pro-Satan even after he personally made it known to me how much he hated me.

Vietnam is etched into my life and causes a lot of pain in very demeaning ways. I was fortunate to travel back to Vietnam under Dave Reaver Wounded Warriors Ministries in 2016. I went with several other warriors who had been wounded in Vietnam. The first time I had gone to Vietnam, I took my M-16 rifle in my hand to kill; on this trip, I took John 3:16 in my heart and my Bible in my hand to heal. It was a supernatural experience. I preached the good news of Jesus to my Vietnam brothers and sisters and was ministered to through them as well.

The most heartbreaking time came when I met a former Viet Cong soldier and a North Vietnamese soldier who had become born-again children of God. We greeted one another with tears and expressions of forgiveness. I am still struck deep in my heart by how I had once hated them as my enemies and wanted to kill them—two wonderful men I never knew, worlds apart, but I had enough hatred in my heart to kill them. War is evil—supposedly civilized human beings trying to kill one another whom they had never met or argued with over anything. I often weep with dismay at how human beings can be driven to kill one another without cause when together they could add value to each other for the greater good. That's why I have been on a mission to share Jesus, the only hope for all humanity.

While serving as a federal agent and now a born-again child of God, I wanted to run from God and be more active in my law enforcement career as a Christian. I was running because God called me to pastor, and I did not want to submit to that call, so I rebelled against Him. I thought I could convince God to see things my way; after all, I would still be a Christian and go to church. So I volunteered to work undercover narcotics in Chicago as I had worked as a police officer and had enjoyed it. I was driven by that dangerous life; my adrenaline high was deceiving me into thinking I could not have a fulfilled life without it. I was fooling myself thinking that I could do the job without indulging in the lifestyle required to operate successfully.

While out trying to establish a connection, I was "made" by an individual and confronted. I had to engage in lying, and I began to drink alcohol to prove I belonged. I overstepped my guards and quickly regressed to a lifestyle I had experienced as an undercover police detective several years earlier.

I felt such guilt and shame before God, and my past guilt of Vietnam compounded that. I could barely breathe as a result of the heaviness on my heart, and I returned to my apartment alone. I walked through the door with tears in my eyes, and I fell to my knees weeping due to my guilt and shame. I cried myself to sleep and woke up early the next morning with the continued heaviness of guilt and shame; I was trying to figure out what had happened.

I started to the kitchen to get a cup of coffee when I heard, *You have sinned against God. You have failed, and God does not know you anymore. The only thing you can do is kill yourself.* I did not respond verbally but started weeping. I headed to a floor-to-ceiling window. I recall being convinced by the voice as I focused on the window. Seated on the windowsill, I looked down from the fourteenth floor to see if there was an awning that would break my fall when I pushed myself out the window. I did not consider what I was doing, but I needed to obey the voice telling me to kill myself.

I was in the fetal position in the window preparing to thrust my body through it so my head would strike the pavement first guaranteeing my death. I was not conscious of anything or anyone else other than Satan telling me to kill myself. But I suddenly heard, *Zollie! Zollie! Get off that windowsill!* I immediately jumped off the windowsill in a shocked response to see who was there. No one was physically there. I realized I had heard God's voice. I was in total shock at the turn of events.

God then instructed me to call my supervisor and tell him that I could no longer do the job and that I had to return home immediately. I did exactly as I was told. Without any detailed questioning, my supervisor agreed to release me to return home. After getting home, I felt the shame and embarrassment unto God and my family. How could I have been so stupid and blind to have run from God?

I fasted and prayed with deep conviction and repentance because I had failed God. I wept and cried for forgiveness, and God honored my repentance. He forgave me, and I realized the seriousness of the warfare I was in. I studied Jonah and his rebellion against God and wondered how I had fallen into the same trap of running from God.

I studied David and learned from Him God's great desire to receive our confessions of repentance and forgive us. I must say God's discipline is not pleasant, but it is a demonstration of His love. I am convinced I have a thorn in the flesh to keep me humble. It is not something to boast about, but I have learned that it is necessary for my salvation. My biggest challenge is protecting myself from myself. I thank God for it because it keeps me focused on Jesus. I challenge you not to run from God but to Him.

Let me share another major, life-changing event in my life. Two years later while I was praying, God spoke to me again in His attention-getting voice and told me to resign from my job as a federal agent and become a full-time pastor—a stunning challenge. I was a young dad with a young wife and two daughters. I was earning $46,000 a year and living a wonderful life. The young church we had just started could afford to pay me only $3,600 a year.

I shared the news with my wife, and she looked me in my face and said, "Zollie, you know I'll support you, but make sure you're hearing from God." I said OK and immediately went back to my prayer closet to continue my conversation with God. I told Him that I knew He had blessed me with my college degree so I could support my family. He gently interrupted me with simple but powerful words: *I spared your life in Vietnam so that through you, many might come to know me.* I took what He said to heart and resigned from my job. I had learned a very important lesson from my last failure, and I was not going to repeat it.

To this day, I will not demean any of the saints such as Jonah, Thomas, or Peter for acting on their own. Running from God was costly, but it showed me the love God had for me. Since the tragic event in Chicago, I learned God tests us so we can see where we are in our relationship with Him. I can now say without reservation, "Obedience is better than sacrifice" (1 Samuel 15:22 KJV).

By God's grace, I vowed never to dishonor Him again because He had shown His grace to me without measure, more than I deserved. I see my life story plainly shaped out of the creation story—the blessings, the failures, and the restorations. God has clothed us in His undeserved love, and when we experience it, our souls are transformed. I pray that everyone will experience God that way.

My life experiences align with those of all humans; we are all challenged by sin, and unfortunately, many are perishing without Jesus. I was not destroyed because of God's love for me and the grace He has extended to me; I responded to that by surrendering my life to Him through Jesus and becoming one of His born-again children. Some are being destroyed because they do not have a father-and-child relationship with God as I do, but they still have a way out through Jesus, our Lord and Savior, who sets us all free. He is still there for those who are perishing, which is why those of us who have a genuine relationship with God need to show our compassion for the perishing by introducing them to God's Son, Jesus, so they too can be set free.

God is willing that no one perish as stated in 2 Peter 3:9 (KJV): "The Lord is not slack concerning his promise, as some men count slackness;

but is long-suffering to us-ward, not willing that any should perish, but that all should come to repentance." This truth should challenge all of us who are born-again children of God. We must possess our Father's heart as it relates to those who are perishing in their sins. They are His children as well; they just need our help to get back home.

We know that the resolve to not sin is doing good, so let us do good and reach out to those who are perishing. We know that good exists only through the presence of Jesus, so let's share Jesus like a wildfire spreads—not stopping or slowing down for anything. No one deserves the lake of fire without an invitation to receive or reject Jesus. Do you agree? We must become difference-makers!

We are all familiar with this great truth in John 3:16: "For God loved the world so much that he gave his one and only Son, so that everyone who believes in him will not perish but have eternal life." What is significant here is the love of God being expressed as the driving force behind His giving His only begotten Son, Jesus, on behalf of all humanity. God's agape love gives all it has and expects nothing in return.

The only requirement to possess Jesus is to believe in Him and confess Him as your Lord and Savior. As easy as that sounds, people need help to arrive at the place of belief. They need you with your heart of compassion to help them turn from sin to a new life in Jesus. Jesus is the only antidote to rescue one from escaping eternal damnation in the lake of fire and inheriting His promise of eternal life. I so desire to see and be in the presence of God the Father, Jesus, His Son, the Holy Spirit, the comforter, and you, my brothers and sisters, born-again children of God!

We are warriors called to rescue souls from eternal damnation and lead them to eternal life. Let's do it together because we are willing that none perish!

You can make a difference because you are God's blessing to all humanity—so start blessing by sharing your story *that none perish.*

God loves you, so you can love Him, yourself, and others!

REJOICE IN THE LORD AND AGAIN I SAY REJOICE!

SCRIPTURE INDEX BY CHAPTER

Chapter 1

And the judgment is based on this fact: God's light came into the world, but people loved the darkness more than the light, for their actions were evil. (John 3:19)

Chapter 7

Christ is the visible image of the invisible God. He existed before anything was created and is supreme over all creation, for through him God created everything in the heavenly realms and on earth. He made the things we can see and the things we can't see—such as thrones, kingdoms, rulers, and authorities in the unseen world. Everything was created through him and for him. He existed before anything else, and he holds all creation together. (Colossians 1:15–17)

Loving God means keeping His commandments, and His commandments are not burdensome. (1 John 5:3)

Remember to observe the Sabbath day by keeping it holy. You have six days each week for your ordinary work, but the seventh day is a Sabbath day of rest dedicated to the LORD your God. On that day no one in your household may do any work. This includes you, your sons and daughters, your male and female servants, your livestock, and any foreigners living among you. For in six days the LORD made the heavens, the earth, the sea, and everything in them; but on the seventh day he rested. That is why the LORD blessed the Sabbath day and set it apart as holy. (Exodus 20:8–11)

STOP

Chapter 10

Then hear from heaven where you live, and forgive. Give your people what their actions deserve, for you alone know each human heart. (1 Kings 8:39)

But the LORD said to Samuel, "Don't judge by his appearance or height, for I have rejected him. The LORD doesn't see things the way you see them. People judge by outward appearance, but the LORD looks at the heart." (1 Samuel 16:7)

But God removed Saul and replaced him with David, a man about whom God said, 'I have found David son of Jesse, a man after my own heart. He will do everything I want him to do. (Acts 13:22)

Yes, just as you can identify a tree by its fruit, so you can identify people by their actions. (Matthew 7:20)

Chapter 11

Then the LORD God formed the man from the dust of the ground. (Genesis 2:7)

Behold my hands and my feet, that it is I myself: handle me, and see; for a spirit hath not flesh and bones, as ye see me have. (Luke 24:39 KJV)

For God is Spirit, so those who worship him must worship in spirit and in truth. (John 4:24)

Exodus 33:20–23

Chapter 14

1 John 3:8

John 8:44

James 4:7

Jesus told him, "I am the way, the truth, and the life. No one can come to the Father except through me." (John 14:6)

And you will know the truth, and the truth will set you free. (John 8:32)

Matthew 4:1–11

One day the members of the heavenly court came to present themselves before the LORD, and the Accuser, Satan, came with them. Where have you come from?" the LORD asked Satan. Satan answered the LORD, "I have been patrolling the earth, watching everything that's going on." Then the LORD asked Satan, "Have you noticed my servant Job? He is the finest man in all the earth. He is blameless—a man of complete integrity. He fears God and stays away from evil. Satan replied to the LORD, "Yes, but Job has good reason to fear God.

You have always put a wall of protection around him and his home and his property. You have made him prosper in everything he does. Look how rich he is! But reach out and take away everything he has, and he will surely curse you to your face!" "All right, you may test him," the LORD said to Satan. "Do whatever you want with everything he possesses, but don't harm him physically." So Satan left the LORD's presence. (Job 1:6–12)

If we claim we have no sin, we are only fooling ourselves and not living in the truth. But if we confess our sins to him, he is faithful and just to forgive us our sins and to cleanse us from all wickedness. If we claim we have not sinned, we are calling God a liar and showing that his word has no place in our hearts. (1 John 1:8–10)

For I was born a sinner—yes, from the moment my mother conceived me. (Psalm 51:5)

For everyone has sinned; we all fall short of God's glorious standard. (Romans 3:23)

For the wages of sin is death, but the free gift of God is eternal life through Christ Jesus our Lord. (Romans 6:23)

Chapter 15

When Jesus was still some distance away, the man saw him, ran to meet him, and bowed low before him. With a shriek, he screamed, "Why are you interfering with me, Jesus, Son of the Most High God? In the name of God, I beg you, don't torture me!" For Jesus had already said to the spirit, "Come out of the man, you evil spirit." Then Jesus demanded, "What is your name?" And he replied, "My name is Legion, because there are many of us inside this man." Then the evil spirits begged him again and again not to send them to some distant place. There happened to be a large herd of pigs feeding on the hillside nearby. Send us into those pigs," the spirits begged. "Let us enter them." So Jesus gave them permission. The evil spirits came out of the man and entered the pigs, and the entire herd of 2,000 pigs plunged down the steep hillside into the lake and drowned in the water." (Mark 5:6–13)

Chapter 16

1 Corinthians 15:51–58

Luke 12:51–53

But I would have you know that the head of every man is Christ; and the head of the woman *is* the man; and the head of Christ *is* God. (1 Corinthians 11:3 KJV)

Wives, submit to your husbands, as is fitting for those who belong to the Lord. Husbands, love your wives and never treat them harshly. (Colossians 3:18–19)

Titus 2:4–5

In the same way, husbands ought to love their wives as they love their own bodies. For a man who loves his wife actually shows love for himself. (Ephesians 5:28)

1 Peter 1:3–12

1 Peter 3:13–22

Dear friends, don't be surprised at the fiery trials you are going through, as if something strange were happening to you. Instead, be very glad—for these trials make you partners with Christ in his suffering, so that you will have the wonderful joy of seeing his glory when it is revealed to all the world. So be happy when you are insulted for being a Christian, for then the glorious Spirit of God rests upon you. If you suffer, however, it must not be for murder, stealing, making trouble, or prying into other people's affairs. But it is no shame to suffer for being a Christian. Praise God for the privilege of being called by his name! So if you are suffering in a manner that pleases God, keep on doing what is right, and trust your lives to the God who created you, for he will never fail you. (1 Peter 4:12–16, 19)

In the same way, you wives must accept the authority of your husbands. Then, even if some refuse to obey the Good News, your godly lives will speak to them without any words. They will be won over In the same way, you husbands must give honor to your wives. Treat your wife with understanding as you live together. She may be weaker than you are, but she is your equal partner in God's gift of new life. Treat her as you should so your prayers will not be hindered. (1 Peter 3:1, 7)

Chapter 18

Romans 7:16–23

Beware of false prophets, which come to you in sheep's clothing, but inwardly they are ravening wolves. Ye shall know them by their fruits. Do men gather grapes of thorns, or figs of thistles? Even so every good tree bringeth forth good fruit; but a corrupt tree bringeth forth evil fruit. (Matthew 7:15–20)

Chapter 19

Nevertheless we, according to His promise, look for new heavens and a new earth in which righteousness dwells. Therefore, beloved, looking forward to these things, be diligent to be found by Him in peace, without spot and blameless; and consider *that* the longsuffering of our Lord *is* salvation. (2 Peter 3:13–15 KJV)

In fact, according to the law of Moses, nearly everything was purified with blood. For without the shedding of blood, there is no forgiveness. (Hebrews 9:22)

… and from Jesus Christ. He is the faithful witness to these things, the first to rise from the dead, and the ruler of all the kings of the world. All glory to him who loves us and has freed us from our sins by shedding his blood for us. (Revelation 1:5)

But you will receive power when the Holy Spirit comes upon you. And you will be my witnesses, telling people about me everywhere—in Jerusalem, throughout Judea, in Samaria, and to the ends of the earth. (Acts 1:8)

Ephesians 6:10–18

Don't let evil conquer you, but conquer evil by doing good. (Romans 12:21)

Galatians 5:22–26

But the Holy Spirit produces this kind of fruit in our lives: love, joy, peace, patience, kindness, goodness, faithfulness, gentleness, and self-control. There is no law against these things! Those who belong to Christ Jesus have nailed the passions and desires of their sinful nature to his cross and crucified them there. Since we are living by the Spirit, let us follow the Spirit's leading in every part of our lives. Let us not become conceited, or provoke one another, or be jealous of one another. (Galatians 5:22–26)

And now, dear brothers and sisters, one final thing. Fix your thoughts on what is true, and honorable, and right, and pure, and lovely, and admirable. Think about things that are excellent and worthy of praise. (Philippians 4:8)

Instead, let the Spirit renew your thoughts and attitudes. Put on your new nature, created to be like God—truly righteous and holy. (Ephesians 4:23–24)

Don't lie to each other, for you have stripped off your old sinful nature and all its wicked deeds. Put on your new nature, and be renewed as you learn to know your Creator and become like him. (Colossians 3:9–10)

Don't copy the behavior and customs of this world, but let God transform you into a new person by changing the way you think. Then you will learn to know God's will for you, which is good and pleasing and perfect. (Romans 12:2)

Chapter 20

Then He will also say to those on the left hand, 'Depart from Me, you cursed, into the everlasting fire prepared for the devil and his angels. (Matthew 25:41 NKJV)

Then I saw an angel coming down from heaven, having the key to the bottomless pit and a great chain in his hand. He laid hold of the dragon, that serpent of old, who is *the* Devil and Satan, and bound him for a thousand years; and he cast him into the bottomless pit, and shut him up, and set a seal on him, so that he should deceive the nations no more till the thousand years were finished. But after these things he must be released for a little while. (Revelation 20:1–3 NKJV)

2 Timothy 3:1–5

Luke 21:8–19

Mark 10:28–30

John 15:18–19

Just as you sent me into the world, I am sending them into the world. And I give myself as a holy sacrifice for them so they can be made holy by your truth. (John 17:18–19)

1 John 2:15–17 *Stop*

For all who are led by the Spirit of God are children of God. (Romans 8:14)

And I will ask the Father, and he will give you another Advocate, who will never leave you. He is the Holy Spirit, who leads into all truth. The world cannot receive him, because it isn't looking for him and doesn't recognize him. But you know him, because he lives with you now and later will be in you. (John 14:15–17)

But you will receive power when the Holy Spirit comes upon you. And you will be my witnesses, telling people about me everywhere—in Jerusalem, throughout Judea, in Samaria, and to the ends of the earth. (Acts 1:8)

On the day of Pentecost all the believers were meeting together in one place. Suddenly, there was a sound from heaven like the roaring of a mighty windstorm, and it filled the house where they were sitting. Then, what looked like flames or tongues of fire appeared and settled on each of them. And everyone present was filled with the Holy Spirit and began speaking in other languages, as the Holy Spirit gave them this ability. (Acts 2:1–4)

But you have received the Holy Spirit, and he lives within you, so you don't need anyone to teach you what is true. For the Spirit teaches you everything you need to know, and what he teaches is true—it is not a lie. So just as he has taught you, remain in fellowship with Christ. (1 John 2:27)

These things dominate the thoughts of unbelievers, but your heavenly Father already knows all your needs. Seek the Kingdom of God above all else, and live righteously, and he will give you everything you need. (Matthew 6:32–33)

Since we know that Christ is righteous, we also know that all who do what is right are God's children. (1 John 2:29)

See how very much our Father loves us, for he calls us his children, and that is what we are! But the people who belong to this world don't recognize that we are God's children because they don't know him. Dear friends, we are already God's children, but he has not yet shown us what we will be like when Christ appears. But we do know that we will be like him, for we will see him as he really is. (1 John 3:1–2)

Those who have been born into God's family do not make a practice of sinning, because God's life is in them. So they can't keep on sinning, because they are children of God. So now we can tell who are children of God and who are children of the devil. Anyone who does not live righteously and does not love other believers does not belong to God. (1 John 3:9–10)

Everyone who believes that Jesus is the Christ has become a child of God. And everyone who loves the Father loves his children, too. We know we love God's children if we love God and obey his commandments. (1 John 5:1–2)

Dear friend, don't let this bad example influence you. Follow only what is good. Remember that those who do good prove that they are God's children, and those who do evil prove that they do not know God. (3 John 1:11)

Therefore, if anyone *is* in Christ, *he is* a new creation; old things have passed away; behold, all things have become new. (2 Corinthians 5:17 NKJV)

Jesus turned around, and when he saw her he said, "Daughter, be encouraged! Your faith has made you well." And the woman was healed at that moment. (Matthew 9:22)

Then Jesus said to the disciples, "Have faith in God. I tell you the truth, you can say to this mountain, 'May you be lifted up and thrown into the sea,' and it will happen. But you must really believe it will happen and have no doubt in your heart. I tell you, you can pray for anything, and if you believe that you've received it, it will be yours." (Mark 11:22–24)

And the Holy Spirit helps us in our weakness. For example, we don't know what God wants us to pray for. But the Holy Spirit prays for us with groanings that cannot be expressed in words. And the Father who knows all hearts knows what the Spirit is saying, for the Spirit pleads for us believers in harmony with God's own will. (Romans 8:26–27)

This Good News tells us how God makes us right in his sight. This is accomplished from start to finish by faith.

As the Scriptures say, "It is through faith that a righteous person has life." (Romans 1:17)

Can we boast, then, that we have done anything to be accepted by God? No, because our acquittal is not based on obeying the law. It is based on faith. So we are made right with God through faith and not by obeying the law. (Romans 3:27–28)

So then faith *cometh* by hearing, and hearing by the word of God. (Romans 10:17 KJV)

Because of the privilege and authority God has given me, I give each of you this warning: Don't think you are better than you really are. Be honest in your evaluation of yourselves, measuring yourselves by the faith God has given us. (Romans 12:3) STOP

For we walk by faith, not by sight. (2 Corinthians 5:7 KJV)

And it is impossible to please God without faith. Anyone who wants to come to him must believe that God exists and that he rewards those who sincerely seek him. (Hebrews 11:6)

In hope of eternal life, which God, that cannot lie, promised before the world began. (Titus 1:2 KJV)

That being justified by his grace, we should be made heirs according to the hope of eternal life. (Titus 3:7 KJV)

… which come from your confident hope of what God has reserved for you in heaven. You have had this expectation ever since you first heard the truth of the Good News. (Colossians 1:5)

All praise to God, the Father of our Lord Jesus Christ. It is by his great mercy that we have been born again, because God raised Jesus Christ from the dead. Now we live with great expectation, and we have a priceless inheritance—an inheritance that is kept in heaven for you, pure and undefiled, beyond the reach of change and decay. and through your faith, God is protecting you by his power until you receive this salvation, which is ready to be revealed on the last day for all to see. (1 Peter 1:3–5)

So think clearly and exercise self-control. Look forward to the gracious salvation that will come to you when Jesus Christ is revealed to the world. (1 Peter 1:13)

Luke 6:35–36

So you have not received a spirit that makes you fearful slaves. Instead, you received God's Spirit when he adopted you as his own children. Now we call him, "Abba, Father." For his Spirit joins with our spirit to affirm that we are God's children. And since we are his children, we are his heirs. In fact, together with Christ we are heirs of God's glory. But if we are to share his glory, we must also share his suffering. (Romans 8:15–17)

One day an expert in religious law stood up to test Jesus by asking him this question: "Teacher, what should I do to inherit eternal life?" Jesus replied, "What does the law of Moses say? How do you read it?" The man answered, "'You must love the LORD your God with all your heart, all your soul, all your strength, and all your mind.' And 'Love your neighbor as yourself.'" "Right!" Jesus told him. "Do this and you will live!" (Luke 10:25–28)

Love your enemies! Do good to them. Lend to them without expecting to be repaid. Then your reward from heaven will be very great, and you will truly be acting as children of the Most High, for he is kind to those who are unthankful and wicked. You must be compassionate, just as your Father is compassionate. (Luke 6:35–36)

The Spirit itself beareth witness with our spirit, that we are the children of God. (Romans 8:16 KJV)

Ephesians 4:30

1 Thessalonians 5:19

Luke 12:10

I tell you the truth, all sin and blasphemy can be forgiven, but anyone who blasphemes the Holy Spirit will never be forgiven. This is a sin with eternal consequences. (Mark 3:28–29)

And so, dear brothers and sisters, I plead with you to give your bodies to God because of all he has done for you. Let them be a living and holy sacrifice—the kind he will find acceptable. This is truly the way to worship him. Don't copy the behavior and customs of this world, but let God transform you into a new person by changing the way you think. Then you will learn to know God's will for you, which is good and pleasing and perfect. (Romans 12:1–2)

Revelation 12:11

Jesus replied, "The most important commandment is this: 'Listen, O Israel! The LORD our God is the one and only LORD. And you must love the LORD your God with all your heart, all your soul, all your mind, and all your strength.' The second is equally important: 'Love your neighbor as yourself.' No other commandment is greater than these." (Mark 12:29–31)

And we can be sure that we know him if we obey his commandments. If someone claims, "I know God," but doesn't obey God's commandments, that person is a liar and is not living in the truth. But those who obey God's word truly show how completely they love Him. That is how we know we are living in Him. Those who say they live in God should live their lives as Jesus. (1 John 2:3–6)

1 John 4:7–11

We know we love God's children if we love God and obey his commandments. Loving God means keeping his commandments, and his commandments are not burdensome. (1 John 5:2–3)

Love means doing what God has commanded us, and he has commanded us to love one another, just as you heard from the beginning. (2 John 1:6)

But God showed his great love for us by sending Christ to die for us while we were still sinners. And since we have been made right in God's sight by the blood of Christ, he will certainly save us from God's condemnation. For since our friendship with God was restored by the death of his Son while we were still his enemies, we will certainly be saved through the life of his Son. So now we can rejoice in our wonderful new relationship with God because our Lord Jesus Christ has made us friends of God. (Romans 5:8–11)

John 3:16

After saying all these things, Jesus looked up to heaven and said, "Father, the hour has come. Glorify your Son so he can give glory back to you. For you have given him authority over everyone. He gives eternal life to each one you have given him. And this is the way to have eternal life—to know you, the only true God, and Jesus Christ, the one you sent to earth. (John 17:1–3)

Fight the good fight for the true faith. Hold tightly to the eternal life to which God has called you, which you have confessed so well before many witnesses. (1 Timothy 6:12)

I give them eternal life, and they will never perish. No one can snatch them away from me, for my Father has given them to me, and he is more powerful than anyone else. No one can snatch them from the Father's hand. The Father and I are one. (John 10:28–30)

ABOUT THE AUTHOR

Zollie L. Smith joined the US Army after graduating from high school, was trained as an airborne infantryman, served fifteen months in Vietnam, and was awarded the Bronze Star Medal and the Purple Heart. After his service, Smith earned several degrees, diplomas, and designations and worked in a variety of careers, including as a police officer and detective, postal inspector, senior pastor, assistant district superintendent and executive director of U.S. Missions Assemblies of God. He and his wife, Phyllis, have six daughters.

CPSIA information can be obtained
at www.ICGtesting.com
Printed in the USA
BVHW071344310721
612754BV00004B/6